Gin Das Winan
Documenting Aboriginal History
in Ontario

Gin Das Winan
Documenting Aboriginal History
in Ontario

A Symposium at Bkejwanong, Walpole Island
First Nation, September 23, 1994

Sponsored by the Champlain Society

Hosted by Nin.Da.Waab.Jig
Walpole Island First Nation Heritage Centre

Occasional Papers
Number 2

Edited by
Dale Standen and David McNab

Toronto
Published by the Champlain Society
with the assistance of the Government of Ontario
through the Ministry of Citizenship, Culture and Recreation

Canadian Cataloguing in Publication Data

Main entry under title:

Gin das winan: documenting aboriginal history in Ontario: a symposium at Bkejwanong, Walpole Island First Nation, September 23, 1994

(Occasional papers; no.2)
1st ed.
Includes bibliographical references.
ISBN 0-9693425-6-X

1. Indians of North America—Ontario—History—Sources—Congresses. 2. Oral history—Ontario—Congresses. I. Standen, Dale, 1942- II. McNab, David, 1947- III. Champlain Society. IV. Series: Occasional papers (Champlain Society); no.2.

E78.O5G54 1996   971.3'00497   C96-900077-4

Typesetting by Trent University Design Office
Printed and bound in Canada by Commercial Press

The Champlain Society
P.O. Box 592, Station R
Toronto, Ontario
M4G 4E1

Printed on acid-free paper

Table of Contents

Preface

The essays in this collection of occasional papers are a selection from those given at the symposium "Documenting Aboriginal History in Ontario" held at Walpole Island First Nation on September 23, 1994. Sponsored by the Champlain Society and assisted by a generous grant from the Ministry of Citizenship, Culture, and Recreation, the symposium enjoyed the warm hospitality of Nin.Da.Waab.Jig, Walpole Island First Nation Heritage Centre, and the community of Bkejwanong.

Translated into English, Nin.Da.Waab.Jig means "those who seek to find," a most appropriate expression to describe the spirit in which the symposium was conceived. The work of the Heritage Centre under the leadership of Executive Director Dean Jacobs is renowned. The Centre's publication, *Walpole Island: The Soul of Indian Territory* (1987), which received the Ontario Historical Society's Joseph Brant Award, is of special significance for this symposium. As historian Donald Smith observed, it is a book "about an Indian community, and written from the inside by its members," which makes it "extremely valuable.... The oral testimony of older band members adds an important dimension to the study." Oral tradition as a source for documenting Aboriginal history is a prominent theme of the symposium.

Throughout its existence the Champlain Society has taken a keen interest in the history of the First Nations of Ontario and Canada. Many of the Society's ninety-two volumes of documents relating to Canadian history are rich sources for Aboriginal history. They include *Sagard's Long Journey to the Country of the Hurons; Customs of the American Indians Compared with the Customs of Primitive Times by Father Joseph François Lafitau; The Valley of the Six Nations;* and the numerous journals and letters of officials, voyageurs, traders and explorers in virtually all parts of what was to become Canada. Beyond these noteworthy publications, various recent and current members of the Champlain Society's Council – Jennifer Brown, Conrad Heidenreich, Douglas Leighton, David McNab, Sylvia Van Kirk, Morris Zaslow – have made major contributions to our understanding of the history of our country's Aboriginal peoples. They and others have joined Aboriginal scholars in helping to give the history of Canada's First Nations the wider recognition it deserves.

From its inception in 1905 until recently, the Champlain Society restricted its activities to publishing beautifully produced and splendidly edited volumes of documentary history. In so doing the Society came to be perceived by some as a rather stuffy, elitist, scholarly organization with restricted membership. This image, in which there was much truth, is changing dramatically. For some years now membership has been unrestricted in number. The Society has been seeking to expand its educational mission, to play an advocacy role in the preservation of the documentary record, to build new partnerships with others dedicated to preserving heritage, and to sponsor small, focused colloquia such as the one that produced this collection of occasional papers.

On behalf of the Champlain Society I want to express how pleased and grateful we are to Walpole Island First Nation for having so willingly embraced our proposal for a partnership in this symposium, and to the Ministry of Citizenship, Culture and Recreation for judging it worthy of support.

Gerald Killan
Past President, The Champlain Society

Introduction

When we were searching for a title for this collection of essays, Reta Sands of the Nin.Da.Waab.Jig Heritage Committee and expert on the Ojibwa language suggested *Gin Das Winan,* meaning "stories" that provide historical understanding for the Walpole Island First Nation. The term seems especially appropriate because the most notable feature of recent scholarship in Aboriginal history is the primacy given to Aboriginal perspectives.

As Dr. Gerald Killan notes in his preface, the Champlain Society from its beginning has maintained a visible interest in Aboriginal history and published extensive collections of documents essential to an understanding of it. Inevitably, the selection of and approach to these documents reflects historical interests of editors, membership and wider community prevalent at the time of publication. Until the last twenty-five years or so, these interests focused on Euro-Canadian history of British and French experience. Aboriginal perspectives on events were rarely a concern.

Reflecting the increasing cultural and social diversity of Canada in recent decades, mainstream historical interest – both professional and popular – has expanded its focus to include groups and individuals previously relegated to the margins. Ordinary people, labourers, women, ethnic minorities, Aboriginal people, have become the subjects of inquiry in their own right, not as passive subordinates of male, Euro-Canadian public figures, but as agents of their own destinies and influential participants in the larger, common historical experience. The explosive growth of interest in these branches of "social" history coincides with the political assertiveness by self-conscious groups, proud of their identities, who object to being marginalized. New awareness raises vexing questions, answers to which have required specialized methods of discovering and analyzing evidence. Indeed, the nature of evidence in many cases is quite different from the written documentary sources that are the core of most of our history. In no case is this moreso than in Aboriginal history.

It was not possible to publish all the papers presented at the symposium. Nevertheless, those included here represent much of the diversity of documentation that was at the heart of the event. Dean Jacobs' paper introduces us to Bkejwanong, Walpole Island, and to the richness of sources, both textual and oral, that allow him to document the strength of identity of the Bkejwanong community over its long history. Similarly, in his study of treaty fishing rights of the Walpole Island First Nation and of the Saugeen Ojibwa First Nation, Victor Lytwyn illuminates the continuum of First Nations' independent history. Indeed, if there is a common conclusion to be drawn from all papers, it is surely that Aboriginal history is and always has been vibrant within Aboriginal communities. And if until recently this history has been invisible to the Canadian mainstream the reason is a want of looking – more accurately, a want of listening, because the singular source for Aboriginal perspectives on history is oral tradition.

For the Euro-Canadian historical imagination, entrenched in its own tradition of the written word, the continuing presence of Aboriginal oral tradition understandably attracted little attention. The power of oral tradition, as Paul Williams[1] reminds us in his paper, stems from its centrality in Aboriginal culture: it is much more than history with the written word left out. Oral traditions are a cultural tool, the First Nations' way of knowing and understanding themselves and others.[2] To his focus on oral tradition as historical source, Williams adds a discussion of the growing acceptance of oral tradition as an authority in jurisprudence.

Using the case of Chief John Assance, Catherine Sims reminds us how essential are official documentary texts for an understanding of Aboriginal history, and especially how it is possible to interpret non-Aboriginal sources to discover Aboriginal perspectives. Like written documents, material objects and pictorial records relating to Aboriginal history have long been familiar. In the final essay of this collection, Joan Vastokas applies the analytical methods of anthropology and art history to explore the narrative meanings embedded in select pictorial records, especially Ojibwa birch bark scrolls of the Great Lakes area.

Although each of these essays deals primarily with one or two kinds of records of Aboriginal history, they all draw upon the wider diversity of sources available to interpret the meaning of the record at hand, written, oral or pictorial. Whatever questions we bring to the records of the past, the reliability of the answers we find will depend upon our serious attention to all forms of documentation.

With its mission of publishing historical records for public education, the Champlain Society is eager to embrace the widest possible definition of historical records, and to facilitate discussion with members of diverse communities of the value of their particular records for their history. Such a discussion was intended by "Documenting Aboriginal History in Ontario": the symposium fulfilled the Society's highest expectations. We benefited from the knowledge and expertise of our contributors who generously participated in the venture, and from the outstanding organization of Dean Jacobs and the staff of Walpole Island First Nation Heritage Centre. And we especially benefited from the attendance of many of the Bkejwanong community so willing to exchange views with visitors.

Dale Standen, Trent University
David McNab, Toronto

---

1   Although obligations of his legal practice prevented Paul Williams from attending the symposium, we are thankful to be able to publish his paper in this collection.

2   See Simon Schama, *Landscape and Memory*, (Toronto, Random House, 1995) for a thought-provoking argument for the power of memory and landscape in defining culture.

"We have but our hearts and the traditions of our old men": Understanding the Traditions and History of Bkejwanong

Dean M. Jacobs
Executive Director, Nin.Da.Waab.Jig.
Bkejwanong First Nation

Our present-day community is nestled between Ontario and Michigan at the mouth of the St. Clair River. The modern delta emerged only 6,000 years ago. This place is known to us as Bkejwanong, the place where the waters divide. It is also known as Walpole Island, named after the "warpoles", which were long wooden staves planted in the ground with the emblems of the First Nations on them. These warpoles were seen by the early visitors. Bkejwanong has been occupied by Aboriginal people for thousands of years. It is today home to 2,000 Ojibwa, Potawatomi and Ottawa. Having a common heritage we formed the Three Fires Confederacy – a political and cultural compact that has served us well.[1] The "Island" is blessed with a unique ecosystem including 6,900 hectares of the most diverse wetlands in all of the Great Lakes Basin. Actually, Walpole Island consists of six islands with Walpole being the largest. The land portion of the "reserve" contains a total of 58,000 acres. I use the term "reserve" lightly because in fact Walpole Island has never been founded, legislated, established, set apart or surveyed as a "reserve." Walpole Island has the distinction of being "unceded territory." This fact, together with its natural and human resources, makes Walpole Island a very special place.

Walpole Island is also known for its rare flora and fauna. Our local economy is highly diverse and rich. It is dependent on the bounty of the land and its fruits.[2] Our lands and waters still support recreation and tourism. Hunting, fishing and trapping is a multi-million dollar industry in our community. Even though we are the southern-most reserve in Canada citizens of our First Nation, incredibly, can still support their families through hunting, fishing, trapping and guiding activities. These traditional activities are central to our economic base and cultural integrity.

Over the past three hundred years visitors to Bkejwanong have commented on the beauty of our lands and waters. Monsieur de Sabrevois, one of our first visitors, came from France passing through our Territory in 1718:

> Five Leagues from destroit [Detroit] is a small Lake called Ste. elene [Lake St. Clair], which is seven leagues in length and not very Wide, as one sees the land on either side. This lake Is well filled with Fish, especially with

1 Nin.Da.Waab.Jig., *Walpole Island, The Soul of Indian Territory*, Bkejwanong, 1987, especially pp. 126.

2 For an excellent description of the Walpole Island First Nation Territory see Fred Coyne Hamil, *The Valley of the Lower Thames, 1640-1850*, Toronto: University of Toronto Press, 1951, pp. 4-6.

Whitefish.... Twelve Leagues from the fort of destroit, always ascending The River, you will find the Misisaguez [Mississagas] "Sauvages,"[3] who dwell on a beautiful island [Walpole Island] where they have cleared some land. They number about 60 or 80 men. Their language is like The outaouac [Ottawa], with but little difference. Their customs are The same, and they are very industrious....[4]

Alexander McKee, the head of the Indian Department,[5] came to St. Anne Island in 1796 and we entered into a treaty to protect our lands and waters:

> When the White Elk [better known by his "white name" Alexander McKee] finding that our fathers were growing poor and wretched in the vicinity of the Long Knife[6] brought them up to the Island [St. Anne Island] on which you now find us. He left from his canoe with a lighted brand on [in] his hand and after having kindled the first Council Fire which had ever shone upon it, he gave it and to them forever.
>
> "Remain my children," said he. "Do not desert the abode to which I have brought you. I never shall let any one molest you. Should any persons come to ask from you a part of these lands, turn from them with distrust and deny them their request. Never for a moment heed their voice and at your dying day instruct your sons to get theirs, teach them as generation succeeds generation to reserve intact their inheritance and poverty shall be unknown to them...."[7]

3   A modern translation would likely be the Mississauga or the Ojibwa Nation. On the French concept of "Sauvage" see Olive Patricia Dickason, *The Myth of the Savage and the Beginnings of French Colonialism in the Americas*, Edmonton: The University of Alberta Press, 1984, pp. 5-84, especially pp. 61-84.

4   Monsieur de Sabrevois, "1718: Memoir on the Savages of Canada as far as the Mississippi River describing their Customs and Trade," *Wisconsin Historical Collections*, Volume 16: 369-370.

5   Reginald Horsman, "Alexander McKee," *Dictionary of Canadian Biography*, Toronto: University of Toronto Press, Volume IV, 1979: 499-500. See also his *Matthew Elliott, British Indian Agent*, Detroit: Wayne State University, 1964. For a modern study see Colin G. Calloway, *Crown and Calumet, British-Indian Relations, 1783-1815*, Norman: University of Oklahoma Press, 1987, especially pp. 51-76.

6   The Americans were known by the First Nations as Long Knives as a result of the weapons which they used against Aboriginal people in the late eighteenth century. The phrase would mean "in the vicinity of the place where the white Americans live" and likely refers to American territory south and west of Lakes St. Clair and Erie.

7   Jarvis Papers, Baldwin Room, Metropolitan Toronto Public Library, "Speech of the Indian Chief Beyigishigneshkam to Colonel Jarvis on Walpole Island," September 1839. A copy of this document is in Nin.Da.Waab.Jig. files at Bkejwanong.

Our lands have been a special place and this fact was immediately recognized and re-affirmed. The power of our oral tradition has survived to this day to safeguard our Reserve lands and to keep them unceded and intact.

Some visitors encountered opposition when they came to the Island. And when they did not always follow our customs and our laws, they paid the price. In the early 1820's the survey party of the international water boundary between Canada and the United States found this out. One of the party, a British military surgeon, Dr. John J. Bigsby[8] gave this account of the beauty and the dangers within Bkejwanong:

When we arrived we found the scenery here very pretty, the borders of the lake, for miles inland, being a savannah of long, bright green grass, with woods in the rear disposed in capes, islands, and devious avenues. I was delighted, and landed for a run; but to my surprise, I stepped into water ankle-deep, and forthwith returned. But a more serious evil was the bad quality of the water, as we were to be here for several days, and the weather sultry and close. It was tainted and discoloured by the dead bodies of a minute pink insect, and was only drinkable after straining and boiling.... The natural result of all this was sickness.... From this pestilential spot we removed, in the prosecution of our work, to one of the channels in the island of St. Mary near Baldoon, amid aguish meadows of coarse grass ... cultivated after a fashion by various remnants of Indian tribes.

As the place looked very likely for game, and the sailors had little to do, permission was given to four or five of them to beat up with fowling-pieces an open marsh of many hundred acres close to us, with clumps of wood on the higher ground.

Towards evening one of the sporting sailors came running to the schooner, to say that a comrade had shot himself; but he was so breathless and frightened, that he could only point in the direction of the body about a mile off. Three or four of us ran off, and, after a little search, we found the unfortunate man quite dead, lying across his discharged gun, on his face, which was in a pool of blood. The cast-off skin of a snake, beautifully perfect, lay near him. As there was nothing to point to foul play, we supposed that he had struck at the seeming snake with the butt-end of his gun, and that the gun had gone off and lodged its contents in the neck, where we found a small round hole close to his jugular vessels.[9]

---

8   Anthony W. Rasporich, "John Jeremiah Bigsby," *Dictionary of Canadian Biography*, Vol. 11, 1881-1890, Toronto: University of Toronto Press, 1982, pp. 72-73.

9   John J. Bigsby, M.D. *The Shoe and Canoe or Pictures of Travel in the Canadas. Illustrative of their Scenery and of Colonial Life; with Facts and Opinions on Emigration, State Policy, and other Points of Public Interest.* In Two Volumes, London: Published by Chapman and Hall, 1850.

The ignorance of visitors, like learned Dr. Bigsby, who represented the epitome of European-based science, saw Bkejwanong only as a "pestilential spot" filled with disease and death. This is also a theme of our visitors. But we know our lands and waters.

In 1830 we held a Council Fire with William Jones, another Indian agent that the government sent to us. This is what our old men told him about our lands and waters:

> When he [Alexander McKee] first came to this place he said, "you see no houses on this River and there shall be none made by us and where ever you have marked out the land for us, we will remain."
>
> When he came to see us on St. Ann's Island down Baldoon River, he built a fire in front of his Red children and said, "I do not build this [Council] fire before you to take the land from you. It is the fire of friendship. The hands are so strongly put together that no man can part them asunder, and no person shall extinguish it."
>
> When we surrounded the fire of friendship that he had kindled, he again told us that the land was to remain ours, that the words which he now spoke was heard by Him who made us and would be sent to our great father over the waters. As some of our young men were not present, they might come whenever they please and enjoy all that was promised us; and again told us that this land should forever belong to the three tribes. Moreover, he told us that this land is good; even the marshes will yield you plenty. The great River [the St. Clair River watershed which includes the Chenail Ecarte and Big Bear (Sydenham) Rivers] is full of living animals for your use and the Prairies will give you something; therefore, keep it for the use of your three tribes and never part with it.[10]

In the summer of 1836, the Irish-born, feminist traveller Anna Brownell (Jameson) Murphy (the wife of the Attorney General for Upper Canada),[11] described Bkejwanong during her "summer rambles":

> ... we stretched northwards across Lake St. Clair. This beautiful lake, though three times the size of Lake Geneva, is a mere pond compared with the enormous seas in its neighbourhood. About one o'clock we entered the river St.

---

10 National Archives of Canada, RG 10, Indian Affairs Records, Volume 39, "Speech from Cheppewas [Chippewa or Ojibwa] of Walpole Island," dated 12 August 1830.

11 Clara Thomas, "Anna Brownell (Jameson) Murphy," *Dictionary of Canadian Biography*, Volume VIII, 1851-1860, Toronto: University of Toronto Press, 1985, Volume III, pp. 649-651.

Clair, (which, like the Detroit, is rather a strait or channel than a river,) forming the communication between Lake St. Clair and Lake Huron. Ascending
this beautiful river, we had, on the right, part of the western district of Upper
Canada, and on the left the Michigan territory. The shores on either side,
though low and bounded always by the line of forest, were broken into bays
and little promontories, or diversified by islands, richly wooded, and of every
variety of form. The bateaux of the Canadians, or the canoes of the Indians,
were perpetually seen gliding among these winding channels, or shooting
across the river from side to side, as if playing at hide-and-seek among the
leafy recesses. Now and then a beautiful schooner, with white sails relieved
against the green masses of foliage, passed us, gracefully curtseying and sidling
along. Innumerable flocks of wild fowl were disporting among the reedy
islets, and here and there the great black loon was seen diving and dipping, or
skimming over the waters.[12]

By 1839, at a Council Fire with Samuel Peters Jarvis, the head of Indian Affairs
from Toronto, the encroachments of white colonists on our Reserve had become a
bone of contention:

We have no words of ancient treaties to refer to, we have no books handed
down to us by our ancestors to direct us in our speech; we have but our hearts
and the traditions of our old men; they are not deceitful.... You find us still
the same as the old men that he addressed; faithful and ready in our alliance
to our great Mother, but in all other respects, alas how altered. Our lands
have dropped from our hands to those of the white squatter, the clearings we
had made have been born from us to yield their crops to new masters. There
is hardly a foot of ground that we can call our own or hold secure from the
threats & ill deeds of these men. One hundred of our men have been
destroyed, our dogs have been shot at the very doors of our lodges, our horses
have been stolen from us. Father, we have become slaves and we are unhappy....
Some of our Chiefs unmindful of the warning of the White Elk, deaf to the
voice of their fathers have given away our land and with it our happiness.
Vainly have we reproached them with it; our answer has been "This land is
ours." The great Father in Toronto has given us the sole disposal of it....
You have spoken to us about your Great Spirit but the Indian was not

12 Anna Brownell (Jameson) Murphy, Winter Studies and Summer Rambles in Canada, London:
Saunders and Otley, Conduit Street. 1838, Coles Canadiana Collection, Toronto: Coles Publishing
Company, 1970, 1972, Volume 3, pp. 5-6.

made to live like the White man. Our Great Spirit intended us to hunt in the forests for our food, and plan for our subsistence, not for barter or for sale. Father, such is the life we love, we wish for no other God than the God of our forefathers.[13]

Jarvis replied to this speech stating that this "Island which the White Elk brought upon you, and which he promised should be reserved for your benefit, will not be taken from you. It was unwise for you to allow so many white settlers to come among you, and wrong to allow any belonging to the country of the Long Knives. Such people cannot be true friends."[14] Jarvis spent most of his time hunting for sport on Walpole Island. He never returned. He was subsequently found to be embezzling First Nation funds and he was investigated and then fired by the Indian Department. Jarvis never fulfilled his solemn promises to us at our Council Fire to protect our lands and waters.[15]

Moreover, Jarvis wished to assimilate us. He sent us missionaries and told us to become farmers. But we were already horticulturalists. And we had practised agriculture long before the white newcomers reached our territory. We have a Treaty right, promised by Alexander McKee in 1790, to plant and harvest corn.[16]

In the 1840's, some men of the cloth, the black robes, came to Highbanks on our Island. They cut down some of our trees at that place. But it was our place, not theirs. The black robes did not know how to listen and they refused to understand when Chiefs Petwegizhik and Oshawana (John Nahdee) spoke to them:

You, my brother, have books in which you find knowledge that I do not have. You find in them the story of other countries and of ancient times; you find in them many things to educate yourself, and when you speak your knowledge-can be seen. But I do not have the same means to educate myself. And sometimes I feel like a child who knows nothing....

---

13 Jarvis Papers, Baldwin Room, Metropolitan Toronto Public Library, "Speech of the Indian Chief Beyigishigneshkam to Colonel Jarvis on Walpole Island," September 1839.

14 *Ibid.*

15 J.D. Leighton, "The Compact Tory as Bureaucrat: Samuel Peters Jarvis and the Indian Department," *Ontario History*, Volume 73, No. 1, 1981: 40-53. See also for a fuller treatment the author's "The Development of Federal Indian Policy in Canada, 1840-1890," Ph.D Thesis, University of Western Ontario, 1975, especially Chapter V, "The Aftermath of the Jarvis Scandal: The Indian Department 1845-1860." See also the Solomon Youman Chesley Diaries, 1848-1854 in Diaries Collection, Provincial Archives of Ontario, Toronto, MU 839.

16 1797, Upper Canada Land Petitions, Bundle A, 1796-1840, Petition of Sarah Ainse, NAC, Public Records Division, RG 1, L 3, VOL. 3, A Bundle 4, 1796-1798, NO. 45, (Microfilm Reel C-1609), pp. 45c-45d.

We ... know that the Great Spirit created man, and that he gave him a mind to acquire wisdom. We know that he gave him knowledge. We also know that he created other minds that are more wise than ours, more powerful than us, but that are quite inferior to him. I know these truths. The Great Spirit taught them to me through my Ancestor. My way of seeking light is right for me.[17]

The black robes also had to face the consequences for not listening to us, this time with fire. Their mission station, constructed from our sacred oaks, was burned to the ground. They never came back. And they do not live among us.

The nineteenth century Anglican missionary, the Reverend Andrew Jamieson, sometimes understood us. He took time to listen to us. Instead of trying to live on our Island and assimilate us, he moved to Algonac, Michigan and learned our ways and our language.

Almost ten years later, Major John Richardson (1796-1851),[18] the novelist, an Aboriginal person himself, visited us in the Fall of 1848. He published his experiences among us in the *Literary Garland*.[19] Richardson appreciated the beauty of Bkejwanong enormously and he understood us and our stories:

Our trip up the St. Clair was a pleasant one, in regard to weather, as could possibly have been desired. The air had all the softness of mellowed autumn, although the rays of the sun did not penetrate, and impart a golden hue to that peculiar mist, which is so characteristic of the brief season, called Indian summer. Towards evening we entered the channel, which divides Walpole from Herson's Island, and at a somewhat late hour, arrived at an excellent wharf, built by one of the principal Indians on the island, George Rapp – too anglicized a name to be interesting.... The next morning, at an early hour, we descended the St. Clair about two miles, where we came opposite to what is called the Station, on Walpole Island. This we had passed the preceding night, on our way up to Rapp's wharf. The view of the country immediately around the post was exceedingly picturesque.... About nine o'clock in the morning, and as the landing of the presents commenced, the Indians began to assemble from all quarters – many coming from a distance in canoes – but most of them emerging from all points of the wood that skirted the little plain already described, and behind which most of their dwellings were situated. At each moment this increased until twelve o'clock, when nearly the whole were upon the ground, presenting in the variety and brilliancy of their

17 Denys Delage and Helen Hornbeck Tanner (Translator and editor), "The Ojibwa-Jesuit Debate at Walpole Island, 1844," *Ethnohistory*, Vol. 41, Number 2, Spring, 1994: 295-321.

18 David R. Beasley, "John Richardson," *Dictionary of Canadian Biography*, Toronto: University of Toronto Press, 1985, Volume VIII, 1851-1860, pp. 743-747.

costumes in which each seemed to consult his own fancy, a most picturesque spectacle. Scattered around in different small groups, they either stood longing gracefully, or moving over the ground, amused themselves in various ways. Cards and ball-playing engaged their principal attention, but the last was not that spirited game which and once formed a leading characteristic of the Indian race; and yet the men who played were not the half-civilized, and therefore, degenerate beings I had been led to fear I should find, but principally of the original and unadulterated stock of the red man, whose proud demeanour they evidently inherited, and whose language alone, unmixed with that of the white men, was familiar to them. Not the least remarkable for this was Shah-wah-wan-noo, who, notwithstanding five and thirty years had elapsed since the fall of his great leader, during which he had mixed much with the whites, suffered not a word of English to come form his lips. He looked the dignified Indian and the conscious warrior, whom no intercourse with the white man could rob of his native independence of character.

Several of the younger chiefs were gaily enough dressed, and exhibited taste in the costumes they had chosen; but although their leggins were made of the finest scarlet cloth, and these, as well as their garters and moccasins, covered with variegated ribbons of the gaudiest hues, and that the arms of their dark *capots*, were encircled with broad silver bands from the shoulder to the wrist, and that their shirts were of the whitest calico, and their European fashioned beaver hats, ornamented with huge silver rings, in which were stuck the plumes of the ostrich dyed of a jet black color, and tipped with crimson, while from their ears depended multitudinous small drops of a sugar loaf shape.... Most of the Indians on Walpole Island, are what the good Missionary, Mr. Jamieson, terms Pagans, and seemed to me to entertain quite as much contempt for his language as for his creed. These generally are fine athletic looking fellows, whom it will be an object to conciliate in the event of another rupture with the United States.... We remember once hearing a well known, and scrupulously consistent member of Parliament, state in his place, that he so hated the white man – the owner of the worthless acres of this worthless country – and liked the Indian, that if he had half a dozen daughters, he would give them to the latter in preference. Such was almost my own feeling on this occasion.[20]

19 John Richardson, "A Trip to Walpole Island and Port Sarnia.," *Literary Garland*, Volume 7, 1849: 17-26. This paper was reprinted in *Tecumseh and Richardson, The Story of a Trip to Walpole Island and Port Sarnia*, With an Introduction and Biographical Sketch by A.H.U. Colquhoun, Toronto: Ontario Book Company Publishers, 1924.

20 *Ibid.*

In the 1860's, not to be outdone, the Methodists came to proselytize us. Thomas Hurlburt reported his view of us and our land in their organ of propaganda, the *Christian Guardian*.

Walpole Island and vicinity are among the earliest settled parts of Canada. The portions that are sufficiently out of the water to be cultivated are very fertile; but the greater portion of the whole region is made up of sloughs and interminable bogs. The stench from these is intolerable, and the miasma worse than I ever found in any part of the Mississippi region.... All night long clouds of mosquitoes were at the window, and I am serenaded by countless multitudes of bull-frogs, with interludes of cackling, plunging, and splurging of mud-hens, with toads, snakes, and frogs to match. There are bands or belts of timber with marshes between covered with tall waving reeds. It is said that when Sir Francis Bond Head visited these parts, and saw these boundless bogs covered with tall broad-leaved flags and reeds, that he took out some instrument, and, after surveying them for a time, put it up with the remark, "These Indians are very industrious," supposing the whole was Indian corn."[21]

Robert Mackenzie, one of the brothers of Alexander Mackenzie, a Prime Minister of Canada in the 1870's, was sent to us as an Indian agent in the late nineteenth century. He provided a description which emphasized the erroneous fact that we lived in a wilderness and did little or nothing with our lands and waters.[22] The Department of Indian Affairs knew very little about our lands and natural resources. It was even less knowledgeable about us.

We have always had famous visitors from the United States as well. In the early twentieth century, the American capitalist, Henry Ford,[23] was on an early Spring expedition up the St. Clair River through our waters. He misjudged the weather and water conditions and his yacht became entrapped in the ice off our Island. His boat was going to be crushed and he and his companions may have suffered an ill fate had we not rescued him from the ice and took him to safety in our homes. Henry Ford never forgot our kindness. He came back and visited the Front Church along the River, the Church founded by the Reverend Andrew Jamieson. He recognized the potential of our lands and gave us tractors and training in how to use them. He

---

21 Thomas Hurlburt, *The Christian Guardian*, Toronto, June 20, 1864, p. 106.

22 National Archives of Canada, RG 10, Indian Affairs Records, Red (Eastern Series), Volume 1919, File 2835. See also David McNab, "The Walpole Island Indian Band and the Continuity of Indian Claims: An Historical Perspective," in *Nin.Da.Waab.Jig, Occasional Papers*, 1985.

23 See Robert Lacey, *Ford: The Men and the Machine*, London, Heinemann, 1986, pp. 203-204.

wished to assist us in our transition into the technology of the twentieth century. The tractors were intended to replace the fish which were being despoiled in our waters. Henry Ford helped us to move into commercial agriculture.[24]

Our second largest industry is still agriculture. Today, nearly 12,000 acres are under cultivation. Cash crops such as corn and soy bean are mainly produced. Collectively, we farm 4,400 acres under a cooperative we call Tahgahoning (Garden in English) Enterprise. To give you an idea of the size of our farm operation in the early 1980's we purchased the world's largest corn picker. At that time, there were only a handful of these monsters in North America. Ours was the first in Canada.

In 1965, Walpole Island expelled the last Indian agent, the first reserve to do so in Canada, thus opening the door to the modern self-government era. We started at zero level. But we replaced him with one of our own citizens.[25] Bureaucracy is now our third largest industry. Today our workforce numbers well over two hundred. It is what you might call a growth industry. I confess that I am one of those bureaucrats as part of Nin.Da.Waab.Jig. at the Walpole Island Heritage Centre. Nin.Da.Waab.Jig. means "those who seek to find" in our language. This phrase captures the essence of our work. It can further be described as co-operative community-based research.

However all is not right. Today our paradise is under siege. Walpole Island has been subjected to pollutants for decades. First, up-stream is Canada's major petro-chemical and refining region called "Chemical Valley." Between 1974 and 1986, a total of 32 major spills, as well as hundreds of minor ones, involved 10 tonnes of pollutants. Since 1986, the Ontario Ministry of the Environment has recorded an average of 100 spills per year. Second, passing ocean-going freighters are a constant reminder that an "Exxon-Valdez" type of disaster is possible. As it is, these ships are to blame for introducing the menacing and resilient zebra mussels to Lake St. Clair and our wetlands. The purple loosestrife is another prolific foreign invader crowding out everything in its path. If only we could train the zebra mussels to eat purple loosestrife. Third, significant agricultural runoff of pesticides and fertilizers is a major non-point pollution source. Our once popular beaches are closed for weeks on end because of high levels of bacteria. And fourthly, dredging of contamination sediments in the surrounding waters poses yet another serious environmental problem.

---

24 Nin.Da.Waab.Jig. File on Henry Ford. This information was received from the Henry Ford Museum & Greenfield Village, Dearborn, Michigan, enclosed with a letter to me from David R Crippen, Curator of Automotive History at the Museum, dated July 28, 1987. This paragraph is also based on stories from the citizens of Bkejwanong of their encounter with Henry Ford. See also the paper by the Reverend Jim Miller, "The Reverend Simpson Brigham (1875-1926) The Worlds of Henry Ford and Simpson Brigham Collide," presented at the Laurier III Conference, Earth, Water, Air and Fire, held at Bkejwanong, May 13, 1994.

25 Mr. Edsel Dodge who replaced the last Indian agent is now one of our Elders and a member of Nin.Da.Waab.Jig's Heritage Committee.

Environmental degradation has significant implications for our wildlife and its habitat, human health and well being, and economic development, which depends to a large degree on the viability of our natural resource base.

Our social and economic conditions mirror other native communities: high unemployment; high student drop-out rate; substance abuse; family violence; poor housing and ill health. These problems are symptomatic of cultural demise and economic dependency which disrupt the traditional supporting structures of the community and the family.

While the beauty and spirit of Walpole Island is found in its natural resources and people clearly our First Nation faces a great deal of stress. Yet life goes on. The people of Walpole Island view life in a spiritual, holistic and dynamic way. We have a sense of place and community unrivalled in this area of the country. Our Homeland is all we have ever known. It is important for all of us to understand how this fits into the scheme of life. Our story is shared by First Nations from coast to coast: "For Aboriginal people, traditional belief is often expressed by using the circle to represent life. Our life goal can be described as follows: we did not inherit a legacy from our ancestors. We hold it in trust for our future generations."

Here is another way to put it: *sustaining the circle of life*. What can we do to ensure that this happens? First, we can affirm that the goals of Aboriginal people are compatible with the goal of sustainability of the wider society. By working with Aboriginal people sustainability is promoted in the natural resource sector. Second, we ensure the preservation, continued well-being, and development of Aboriginal cultures, including the opportunity for Aboriginal people to determine their own model of development. Third, we foster the sharing of Aboriginal skills and knowledge in a way which contributes to the continued well-being and sustainability of all. The keys to moving towards sustainability are traditional knowledge and self-government. As part of a move towards sustainability, we all must begin to value natural resources more highly, use them more efficiently, and protect them more carefully.

Aboriginal communities have a model of development based on sustainable use of local resources. Aboriginal traditions support this model. Self-government, the settlement of land claims, and the exercise of Aboriginal and treaty rights help Aboriginal people achieve their development goals. Aboriginal initiatives also encourage a structural shift in how our resources are managed. They encourage local management and a sharing of responsibilities for Mother Earth – critical components of sustainability. Aboriginal initiatives also encourage a shift in thinking about how resources are valued and used. Key concepts include sharing, efficient use of resources, and a wider definition of benefits.

Aboriginal people bring skills and knowledge to the development process, in particular, a deep knowledge of local ecosystems. We are in an excellent position to monitor and provide information on local ecosystem health. The juxtaposition of

Aboriginal knowledge and knowledge systems with mainstream European-based science is likely to enrich the world views of all. These include sharing and community use of resources. We bring a holistic worldview in which humans and everyday activities are an intrinsic part of the land and of the maintenance of environmental health. The juxtaposition of these values and ideas with mainstream ideas and values is likely to enrich all of us who share in it. This includes our understanding and our way of telling our history, through our stories. To Aboriginal communities, "the land" has social, cultural, spiritual as well as economic significance. Aboriginal people rely to a significant extent on local resources and the health of their communities and culture is tied in with the health of the local environment, the amount of access they have to resources, the amount of control they have over management of these resources, and the benefits they receive from them.

Aboriginal people have their own history, their own cultures. They have retained values, traditions, and knowledge which are integral to living in harmony with nature. We have a close relationship with the land and its resources which has survived, relatively intact, through centuries of colonization. Those who earn part or all of their livelihood through trapping and other harvesting activities develop a detailed knowledge of wildlife populations and local environmental conditions which is of value to resource monitoring, management and conservation. This detailed knowledge gives Aboriginal people the authority to speak on behalf of the land and to make decisions about the disposition and use of local resources.

Aboriginal people have much to teach the wider population about living in harmony with nature and in community with other people. A strong feature of our cultures is an emphasis on community, on sharing resources through good and bad times, and on group decision-making through consensus. The preservation of the unique cultures of Aboriginal people, and the sharing of their knowledge are therefore an important part of any sustainable life strategy. For this reason one of the indicators of overall sustainability should be the well-being of Aboriginal communities. Recently, our community was the recipient of a major international award, the "We the Peoples: 50 Communities Award."[26] We have now been recognized by the United Nations, in its fiftieth anniversary, as one of fifty communities around the world demonstrating, among other achievements, our commitment to environmental issues. This international recognition comes from our exemplary record in Environmental Research and Sustainable Development Advocacy. In particular, the award is for the leadership role which our community has taken in combining traditional and non-traditional environmental knowledge as the basis for "interacting effectively with the non-indigenous population and western environmental scientists to everyone's mutual benefit."

---

26 This award was presented to us in New York in September, 1995.

In these ways, we are continuing to make our own history within the circle of time. The lands and the waters, their meaning and context, are important in understanding our history. Without it, you will not understand our customs, our language and our laws. European-trained historians have understood the significance of visiting the site of the battle before understanding and interpreting the documents. It is important to see an historical event, indeed, all of history, in a holistic way,[27] which is the way we view our lands and waters.

In Aboriginal history it is critical to have such an approach, for without that experience, our people and our history will not be understood. Our history will not be told accurately. The documents prepared by our visitors over the centuries show us that this is true. The spiritual world of a place[28] is more than land – it is earth, water, air and fire. History, as our Elders continue to tell us, is more than words, more than ink and paper:

When we were created, we were made without those advantages; we have no pen or ink to write, we have nothing but a little piece of flesh called a heart to remember by ....[29]

History is our heart and our soul.

27 See, for example, one of the first environmental histories by a European-trained and educated author Simon Schama, *Landscape and Memory,* Toronto: Random House of Canada, 1995.

28 See Basil Johnston, *The Manitous, The Spiritual World of the Ojibway,* Toronto: Key Porter Books, 1995.

29 National Archives of Canada, RG 10, Indian Affairs Records, Volume 39, "Speech from Cheppewas [Chippewa or Ojibwa] of Walpole Island," dated 12 August, 1830.

Waterworld: The Aquatic Territory of the Great Lakes First Nations

Victor P. Lytwyn, Ph.D.

Introduction:

The Great Lakes of North America have inspired awe and reverence since time immemorial. Ancient pictographs on rocks indicate that the aboriginal peoples who have lived around the Great Lakes held the aquatic world in high esteem. For example, the Agawa Rock Pictographs, located on the northeast shore of Lake Superior, bear silent testimony to the respect of the people for water and the spirits within. Red ochre paintings on the sheer granite face of Agawa Rock depict numerous animal, human and supernatural figures. Among these, fish and animals who live in, under and around the water figure prominently. *Michipeshu*, or the Great Lynx, a supernatural creature who lives underwater, is one of the most enigmatic of the paintings on stone. Thor and Julie Conway described the painting which depicts *Michipeshu* and two giant serpents of Lake Superior as "the ultimate metaphor for Lake Superior – powerful, mysterious, and ultimately very dangerous" (Conway and Conway, 1990: 24).

The danger brought on by storms and waves that can quickly transform the Great Lakes into furious freshwater oceans, is more than counter-balanced by their sheer beauty and magnificent bounty of aquatic resources which have sustained people for thousands of years. The shores of the Great Lakes attracted settlement and the waters facilitated transport and commerce for many First Nations. At the time of first European contact in the 17th century, their were at least 34 First Nations settled around the Great Lakes (Heidenreich and Wright, 1987: 18). Bark canoes, some measuring over 30 feet, capable of carrying up to 18 people, and powered by paddles and sails traversed these water highways (Adney and Chapelle, 1964: 7-13).

The ease of travel throughout the vast Great Lakes drainage basin also facilitated widespread warfare that occasionally erupted between the nations. Although probably aboriginal in origin, warfare escalated after the introduction of European weapons. European colonies in North America also promoted warfare to obtain political and commercial advantages. The rapid growth of the fur trade has been identified as a factor in increasing warfare among the Great Lakes First Nations (Trigger, 1985: 172-225). In 1701, a major peace treaty was ratified at Montreal between the Great Lakes First Nations and the French. The Montreal Treaty, also known as the Grand Settlement, put an end to the incessant warfare and promoted international trade (Havard, 1992: 134-135). It also ushered in a new era of resource sharing among the First Nations. A wampum belt depicting a dish with one spoon, given by the Five Nations Iroquois Confederacy, memorialized the concept of resource sharing[1] (Wallace, 1957: 228).

The 1701 Montreal Treaty did not diminish the proprietary rights or stewardship responsibilities of First Nations for the terrestrial and aquatic resources within

14

their respective territories. Thus, each First Nation would allow others to take resources as long as the harvest did not threaten to usurp their rights of ownership or endanger their management philosophies. First Nations were also willing to allow European newcomers to travel on their waterways[2] and to obtain sustenance from fishing, but they showed no inclination to give up or sell the lakes which were central to their existence.

Contrary to the views of one recent observer, the territorial and resource rights in the Great Lakes did not begin "On Runneymede meadow in June of 1215" (Wright, 1994: 337). The notion that English common law "arrived in the new world with English settlers" (*Ibid: 338*) and gave the newcomers the automatic right to the water and fish in North America is Euro-centric and lacking in historical foundation. Long before the arrival of Europeans, the First Nations were organized societies, and they possessed their own laws and regulations concerning territorial and resource rights. Furthermore, the 1763 British Royal Proclamation affirmed the existing territorial rights of First Nations in North America.

Treaties involving land surrenders negotiated between the First Nations and the British and Canadian governments in 18th and 19th centuries, did not cover the water or aquatic resources in the Great Lakes. While some treaties surrendered certain islands within the lakes, other islands and the fishing grounds around them were specifically retained by the First Nations. The lack of clearly written agreements pertaining to the lakes did not imply that they were considered to belong to no one. In the case of the waters of Lake Huron and Georgian Bay around the Saugeen (Bruce) Peninsula, Queen Victoria issued a Royal Declaration in 1847 acknowledging that the Saugeen Ojibway First Nation held title to their aquatic territory. In other treaties, clearly written agreements on fishing rights implied a continued right to traditional waters around these fishing grounds.

This paper will examine two cases involving Great Lakes First Nations in Canada, and discuss the effect of treaties on existing aboriginal rights in the Great Lakes. The selected cases involve First Nations who signed treaties covering different areas around the Great Lakes. The case of Walpole Island First Nation involves treaties with the British Crown which specifically excluded the waters and islands

---

1   Wampum, or shell beads, strung together forming patterns on belts were valuable gifts which were given at important events such as treaties. The Covenant Chain wampum belt signified the alliance between First Nations and the British. First given by the Five Nations Iroquois Confederacy, it was presented at the 1764 Grand Council at Niagara Falls as a pledge of friendship between all the Great Lakes First Nations and the British. William Johnson, who represented King George III, presented a copy of the 1763 British Royal Proclamation (Anderson, 1847: n.p.).

2   There is evidence to show that First Nations exacted tolls from Europeans who wished to travel across certain waterways. For example, the Kichesipirini Algonquin who lived along the Ottawa River routinely obtained gifts from missionaries and fur traders who used that river. The Rainy River Ojibway also forced fur traders to pay them tolls for using the river as a trade route.

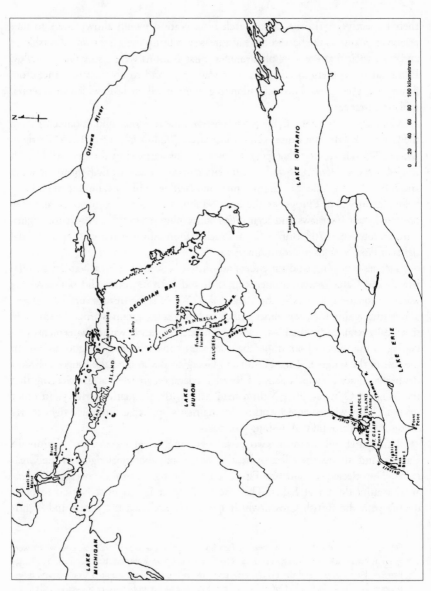

Map by Victor Lytwyn. Lower Great Lakes

connecting Lake Huron and Lake Erie. The case of the Saugeen Ojibway First Nation involves a British treaty and Royal Declaration which recognized the right of the First Nation to the waters and islands in Georgian Bay and Lake Huron around the Saugeen Peninsula.

Walpole Island First Nation:

The waterway connecting Lake Huron and Lake Erie, including the St. Clair River, Lake St. Clair and the Detroit River, is a strategic nexus linking the upper and lower Great Lakes. During the so-called "Beaver Wars" of the 17th century, the area was a pivotal route for controlling the fur trade. During the wars, territorial control shifted between the Five Nations Iroquois Confederacy and the Algonquian nations who had lived in the region since time immemorial. The 1701 Peace Treaty at Montreal ended the period of warfare, and the Chippewa (or Ojibway[3]), Ottawa, Pottawatomi and Wyandotte[4] Nations established villages within the region. The first three nations were known as the Three Fires Confederacy; a coalition which had developed military, economic and political ties. The three nations also spoke similar dialects of the Algonquian language and were intimately connected by cultural traditions. The delta islands in Lake St. Clair, rich in terrestrial and aquatic life, became the major settlement area of the Three Fires Confederacy within the region. The principal village was situated on Walpole Island, the largest of the delta islands.[5]

During the 17th century, the French colonial government sought to extend its territorial claims by issuing proclamations of French sovereignty over large areas of North America. For example, on 23 March 1670, a small party of French traders and missionaries led by Robert Cavalier de La Salle planted a cross at a point somewhere along the northern shore of Lake Erie, and proclaimed possession of the surrounding territory in the name of King Louis XIV. The written document, entitled: "Act of Taking Possession of the Lands of Lake Erie," claimed possession by virtue of the fact that they were the first Europeans to have wintered in that location and because the

---

3   Most of the people prefer the term Anishnabé, meaning original people. The term Chippewa is commonly used by Americans as a tribal designation, but the term Ojibway or Ojibwa is more common in Canada. Chippewa will be used in this study because it was the term most commonly used in the historical documents.

4   The Wyandotte Nation comprised people from the Huron and Petun Nations who had sought refuge among the Three Fires Confederacy after being defeated and driven from their homelands in 1649-50 by the Five Nations Iroquois Confederacy.

5   Archaeological evidence found on Walpole Island indicate that it was inhabited at least 10,000 years ago (Nin.Da.Waab.Jig, 1987: 1). It is apparent that the ancestors of the present-day Walpole Island First Nation built villages in the area in the 17th century A.D. Neal Ferris pointed out that French sources confirm that a village was located near the head of Lake St. Clair at least as early as 1718. This village may have been located on Walpole Island, a point that seems to be confirmed by a number of French sources. Another village may have been located on nearby Harsen's Island (Ferris, 1989: 24).

area was said to be "unoccupied territory" (Lajeunesse, 1960: 8). On 7 June 1687, the French sought to reaffirm their possession of the area between Lake Erie and Lake Huron by issuing a proclamation entitled: "Act of Retaking Possession of the Land in the Neighbourhood of the Strait Between Lakes Erie and Huron" (Lajeunesse, 1960: 12). These ceremonial acts were performed without the knowledge or consent of the Chippewa, Ottawa, Pottawatomi and Wyandotte Nations. Without their agreement, the French proclamations were without foundation. W.J. Eccles pointed out the absurdity of the French claims:

> It is extremely doubtful that the Indians had any understanding of what the ceremony purported. The notion that these strangers could somehow claim to have taken possession of their lands would have seemed utterly ridiculous to them; they might as well have laid claim to the air. As for their now being under the protection of a king thousands of miles away, that too would have appeared nonsensical, since it was obviously the French who required the protection of the Indians in that part of the world. (Eccles, 1984: 485)

The defeat of the French by British military forces and the takeover of the French fort at Detroit in 1760 did not alter the territorial rights of the Walpole Island First Nation. The 1763 British Royal Proclamation prohibited the taking of First Nations lands without a prior formal surrender to the British Crown.[6] One of the first treaties between the Walpole Island First Nation and the British was signed on 19 May 1790. The treaty was held at Detroit between Alexander McKee, who represented the British Crown, and 35 Principal Chiefs of the Chippewa, Ottawa, Pottawatomi and Wyandotte Nations. The geographical boundary of the area covered by the treaty followed a line described as: "the border of Lake Erie and up the Streight [Detroit River] to the mouth of a river known by the name of Channail Ecarte and up the main branch of the said Channail Ecarte to the first fork on the south side" (Canada, 1891, vol. 1: 2). Six years later, on 30 August 1796, McKee met with a number of Chippewa and Ottawa Chiefs on St. Anne Island (NAC, RG 10, vol. 39: 21,652-21,656). The treaty which followed covered a tract of land north of the Thames River, following the left (east) bank of the St. Clair River for about 12 miles to a point marked by a hickory tree (Canada, 1891, vol. 1: 20). A third treaty signed on 26 April 1825 (confirmed on 10 July 1827), covered the land on the left bank of the St. Clair River beginning at the hickory tree and extending north along the shore of Lake Huron (*Ibid: 66*). It is clear from the text of these treaties that the area did

---

6   French settlers who arrived in the region beginning in 1749 were able to obtain titles to river lots granted under the French colonial administration. In addition, several parcels of land in the area around Detroit were obtained by British officers from local Chippewa, Ottawa, Pottawatomi and Wyandotte Chiefs.

not extend into the water or include any islands. The use of the phrase "along the water's edge" signified that the boundary of the area covered by the treaties was not intended to extend into the water.

An examination of transactions involving islands, marshlands and fishing grounds in the St. Clair River, Lake St. Clair and the Detroit River confirms that the aquatic territory was not intended to be included in the treaties. An early transaction involved Fighting Island (also known as Big Turkey Island, or Grosse Isle aux d'Indes). In 1776, ten Pottawatomi Chiefs signed a deed giving title to Fighting Island and a section of land adjacent to the Detroit River to Pierre St. Cosme and his three sons (NAC, RG 10, vol. 325). That deed was challenged by Wyandotte Chiefs who viewed the island and land as belonging to them. The deed was also challenged in 1826 by Thomas Paxton who wished to establish a fishing station on the island. The colonial government in Upper Canada rejected the St. Cosme claim and, in 1827, Paxton obtained a License of Occupation for Fighting Island from Lieutenant Governor Maitland.[7] In an apparently related development, Paxton also agreed to pay an annual rent of $50.00 to the Wyandotte Chiefs (NAC, RG 10, vol. 325).

The Walpole Island First Nation objected to the license given by Upper Canada and to the rent obtained by the Wyandotte Chiefs. The local settlers also complained about Paxton's license, stating that Fighting Island belonged to Walpole Island First Nation who had always allowed them to graze their cattle on the island (NAC, RG 10, vol. 325). In 1829, the Surveyor General was ordered to look into the matter and report back to the Executive Council of the Province of Upper Canada. On August 6, 1829, Acting Surveyor General William Chewett reported that: "no document is to be found in this Office relative to the Indians having made over to the Crown Fighting Island, formerly called Grosse Isle aux D'Inde" (NAC, RG 10, vol. 325). Although Paxton's License of Occupation was upheld, an Order in Council noted that there was an outstanding question of aboriginal title to Fighting Island. The Order in Council stated that:

> The Council upon a consideration of all the documents before them find in them no reason for interfering with the License of Occupation which the Petitioner at present enjoys, but it is not known to the Council that the Island in question has been ever ceded to His Majesty by the Indian proprietors and whether with respect to such Island a License of Occupation should

---

7 Of course, it was the fishing grounds around the Fighting Island and in the Detroit River that were sought after by Paxton. The island alone was of nominal value. In 1826, Thomas Ridout, Surveyor General of Upper Canada, reported that Fighting Island had "very little land fit for tillage and little or no wood, the Indians making it, in summer, a place of encampment and some of them planting a little corn thereon" (NAC, RG 10, vol. 325).

be granted by the Government is respectfully submitted to His Excellency's consideration. (NAC, RG 10, vol. 325)

In 1834, Indian Agent George Ironside investigated the Fighting Island issue and concluded that: "the Islands [in the Detroit River] belong to the Chippewas, Ottawas and Pottawatamies." (NAC, RG 10, vol. 325). Meanwhile, Thomas Paxton attempted to purchase or lease Fighting Island directly from the Walpole Island First Nation Chiefs. One agreement dated 13 June 1836, signed by three Chippewa Chiefs, two Ottawa Chiefs and two Pottawatomi Chiefs, stated that the island was given as a gift to Paxton. Another agreement dated 3 July 1839, signed by Chippewa, Ottawa and Pottawatomi Chiefs, stated that Fighting Island was leased to Thomas Paxton and his heirs for a term of 999 years for a yearly rent of 12 pounds and ten shillings (NAC, RG 10, vol. 325).

While Paxton continued to operate a fishing station on Fighting Island, the government of Upper Canada periodically investigated the issue of title to the island. In 1856, an investigation agreed with a report made about 1827 by James Baby. That report concluded:

I have also to observe that in the Cession made by Ottawas, Chippewas and others in 1791 [1790] – of the large tract of land comprised between Point Pelée called North Toreland and the Chauvanese Township now named Sombra, no mention is made, I believe, of Turkey Island; this may be ascertained from the Deed of Cession now in the Executive Council Office. If not in the Cession the Indian Title is not then extinguished. (NAC, RG 10, vol. 325)

In 1856 Oliver Mowat, already a prominent lawyer in Toronto, wrote a legal opinion on the title to Fighting Island. Mowat agreed with Baby that the island was never surrendered by treaty and therefore aboriginal title continued to exist. However, Mowat found that the Wyandotte Nation had the stronger claim based on their early attempts to drive the St. Cosme family from the island. The Indian Department decided that the best course of action was to sell the island and give the proceeds to the Wyandotte Nation. Prior to the sale, the Indian Department attempted to obtain a treaty of surrender from the Wyandotte Nation. The sale to Paxton for £1,500 took place on 9 December 1858, but the treaty was delayed until 27 February 1863. A patent for Fighting Island was issued to Paxton on 28 June 1867.

On 5 August 1867, the Walpole Island First Nation issued a petition to Governor General Monck. That petition included a statement of title to Fighting Island and other islands in the waters between Lake Huron and Lake Erie. Their title claim was based on the earlier treaties which had specifically left out the islands from any surrender to the British Crown. They also argued that the Wyandottes did not have proprietary rights to the islands because they had been given only a small tract of land to live on by agreement with the Chippewa, Ottawa and Pottawatomi Chiefs.

In 1869, William Spragge, Deputy Superintendent of Indian Affairs, issued a report which concluded that the Wyandotte Nation did not have an exclusive right to Fighting Island. Based on the 1790 Treaty, Spragge found that the Walpole Island First Nation shared in the title to the island. H.L. Langevin, Secretary of State for the government of Canada, acknowledged that Walpole Island First Nation had a right to Fighting Island but refused to re-negotiate the treaty. In a letter to the Chiefs of the Wyandotte Nation, Langevin notified them of the mistake but also cautioned them to take the money without question. He wrote:

> It does not appear that the Wyandotts had at any time a separate and sole right to Fighting Island in the River Detroit, the proceeds of which have been credited to your funds, nor to 'Little Turkey Island' claimed also by you but as yet unsold. And you must distinctly understand that provided you accept as final the present decision the payments on account of Fighting Island will not be disturbed but on that condition you then may retain the purchase money received for the same. (NAC, RG 10, vol. 325)[8]

Other islands were leased by Walpole Island First Nation without the complications that clouded Fighting Island. For example, Peach, or Peche Island, located near the outflow of Lake St. Clair, and Pasture Island [Fawn Island] in the St. Clair River were leased as fishing stations with rental fees paid to Walpole Island First Nation (NAC, RG 10, vol. 776).

Marshlands, especially those surrounding the delta islands in Lake St. Clair, were also leased by the Walpole Island First Nation. In 1875, the Walpole Island First Nation agreed to a conditional surrender of a part of their marshlands for the purpose of leasing the area for "sporting or shooting purposes" (Canada, 1891, vol. 2: 7). In 1895, the Ontario provincial government claimed jurisdiction over the marshlands. Hayter Reed, Deputy Superintendent General of Indian Affairs, rejected Ontario's claim and stated that:

> All the Islands, marsh lands and marshes adjacent to or in the immediate vicinity of Walpole Island, including the portion of land and marsh in question, have long been dealt with by this Department as Indian Lands particularly belonging to the Indians of Walpole Island and rents therefrom have been regularly placed to their credit ... the lands in question are in exactly the same position as Bois Blanc Island, Fighting Island, Turkey Island and all

---

8 In 1941, the deed to Fighting Island was acquired by the Michigan Alkali Company.

others in the waters of the St. Clair River, Lake St. Clair and the Detroit River, which this Department has constantly sold, leased or otherwise administered for the benefit of the Indians. (Walpole Island Heritage Centre, file 10-12)

Although the federal government managed to prevail over Ontario's claim to the marshlands, the lease arrangements came to be viewed as boundary markers of the aquatic territory of Walpole Island First Nation. Negotiations between federal and provincial officials focused on the definition of the edge of the marshlands, or the line of emergent vegetation above the water as a territorial boundary marker. Although the federal Department of Indian Affairs purported to act in their best interests, the Walpole Island First Nation continued to assert that their territory includes the islands, marshlands, water and aquatic resources. On 8 February 1980, Chief Donald Isaac and the Council of Walpole Island First Nation passed a resolution which stated that their territory included all of Lake St. Clair and part of the St. Clair River on the Canadian side of the international boundary (Walpole Island First Nation Council Minutes).

Saugeen Ojibway First Nation:

The Saugeen Ojibway First Nation occupied a large territory including the Saugeen (Bruce) Peninsula and the drainage basins of the Saugeen, Sauble and Sydenham Rivers. They also occupied many islands in Georgian Bay and Lake Huron, and harvested fish in the rich shoals around the islands.[9] Before they signed any treaty with the British Crown, the Saugeen Ojibway First Nation entered into lease agreements for the use of some of their islands and waters. The first agreement was signed in 1834 for the Fishing Islands located about 20 miles north of the mouth of the Saugeen River in Lake Huron. Three "Chiefs of the Chippewa Fisheries," Jacob Metigwab, Alexander Matwayash and John Aisance,[10] signed an agreement with the directors of the Huron Fishing Company (NAC, RG 10, vol. 56: 58,707). That agreement had been ordered by the government of Upper Canada as a pre-requisite for the Company obtaining a License of Occupation (AO, RG 1, A VII, vol. 10: 66).

In 1836, a treaty was signed by several Saugeen Ojibway Chiefs on Manitoulin Island as an apparent ancillary to treaty negotiations between Lieutenant Governor Francis Bond Head and the Manitoulin Chiefs. The area covered by the treaty included about 1.5 million acres south of the Saugeen Peninsula. According to Chief Metigwab, Lieutenant Governor Bond Head promised to protect the Saugeen Ojibway First Nation territory in the peninsula and surrounding waters. Chief

---

9   For a more detailed discussion about the fisheries of the Saugeen Ojibway First Nation see Lytwyn, 1993.

10   Alternatively spelled Assance.

Metigwab stated that Bond Head confirmed "that they the Sahgeeng Indians owned all the islands in the vicinity of that neck or point of land he was about to reserve for them, and that he would remove all the white people who were in the habit of fishing on their grounds."[11] The latter promise was in response to soured relations between the Saugeen Ojibway First Nation and the Huron Fishing Company. By 1836, the Company had reneged on its agreement but continued to fish in the waters around the Fishing Islands.

In 1843, the Saugeen Ojibway Chiefs petitioned the government of Upper Canada to give them a "piece of paper" delineating their territory (NAC, RG 10, vol. 538). Aided by benevolent groups such as the Aborigines Protection Society in London, who were outraged over the terms of the 1836 Treaty, the Saugeen Ojibway First Nation succeeded in obtaining their piece of paper in 1847. On 29 June 1847, a Royal Declaration was issued by Queen Victoria which described the territory of the Saugeen Ojibway. The Declaration stated that the territory included the Saugeen Peninsula and the adjacent islands within a seven mile limit (NAC, RG 68, vol. Liber AG, Special Grants, 1841-1845). It is apparent that the seven mile limit was added to include all the fishing grounds around the peninsula; an object of special concern to the Saugeen Ojibway First Nation at that time.

On 13 October 1854, the Saugeen Ojibway Chiefs signed another treaty with representatives of the British Crown. That treaty surrendered most of the land in the Saugeen Peninsula, saving a few small reserves. However, the treaty specifically excluded the islands and fishing grounds in Lake Huron and Georgian Bay. The treaty document stated that "It is understood that no islands are included in this surrender" (Canada, 1891, vol. 1: 196).

Despite the promises in the Treaty and Royal Declaration, the colonial government in Canada failed to protect the aquatic territory of the Saugeen Ojibway First Nation from intrusions by commercial fishing companies. Although lease arrangements made between the government and the fishing companies provided small rental fees, the Saugeen Ojibway Chiefs sought to reclaim their own jurisdiction. In 1859, the Chiefs met with newly appointed Fishery Overseer William Gibbard and demanded that he refrain from leasing any of their fishing islands (NAC, RG 10, vol. 418: 572). In 1860, the Saugeen Ojibway Chiefs issued a petition to the government complaining about encroachments on their traditional waters:

At the expiration of the present terms of lease we wish to have our Islands and fisheries back for our own use, for although we do not prosecute the fishing

11 A copy of this document was provided by Paul Williams. The original document, entitled: "Statement of Metigwab one of the Sahgeeng Chiefs, made in a General Council held at the River St. Clair on the 13th Sept. 1836," was held in the Six Nations and New Credit Agency files of the Department of Indian Affairs, no. 123-1836.

like the white man, yet we are satisfied that it will be for our interest and advantage to have them for our own use. (Schmalz, 1977: 115)

Gibbard failed to comply with their demands, and instead gave six fishing leases to commercial fish companies. In 1861, the fish companies harvested about 2,500 barrels of fish valued at $10,000 (Canada, SP, 1862: n.p.).

When diplomacy failed, the Saugeen Ojibway and other Great Lakes First Nations resorted to violence to protect their aquatic territory and resources. Fishery Overseer Gibbard reported that the fishing stations on the Fishing Islands were "regularly destroyed by Indians" (Canada, SP, 1862, no. 11: n.p.). In 1863, a group of people from the Wikwemikong First Nation on Manitoulin Island destroyed a fishing station on nearby Lonely Island. Gibbard tried unsuccessfully to arrest the suspects at Wikwemikong, and he was mysteriously murdered about a month after leaving the island.[12] During an investigation of the incident, W.F. Whitcher reported that the Wikwemikong First Nation held strong views about their right to the land and water. He noted that:

In all that relates to soil and fisheries they conceive themselves sovereign proprietors, and, as such, not amenable to the laws and usages which govern subjects of the realm. They make and administer their own laws. Whosoever would occupy their lands, reside within their jurisdiction and use 'their fisheries,' must conform to tribal orders and decrees. As rightful and absolute owners of Lonely Island they think they had the power and right to put away the white occupiers thereof who had rendered themselves obnoxious. (Canada, SP, 1863, no. 18: n.p.)

Whitcher reported that he "argued patiently with them on the fallacy of these pernicious notions," but was unable to convince them otherwise. He advanced the government's position which claimed to be *loco parentis* (standing in parental relationship) to the First Nations.

---

12 Accompanied by 22 constables armed with revolvers, police batons and handcuffs, Gibbard had tried unsuccessfully to apprehend several people at Wikwemikong who were suspected of destroying a commercial fishing station on nearby Lonely Island. However, he arrested another suspect named Oswa-anw-mekee (also known as John Little Thunder) at Bruce Mines, and brought him before Magistrate John Prince at Sault Ste. Marie. Oswa-anw-mekee was released on bail, and made his return to Manitoulin Island aboard the steamship *Ploughboy*. Gibbard was also on board, but he disappeared mysteriously during the night. His body was found washed up on the shore of Manitoulin Island several days later. An inquest determined that he had been murdered, but no one was convicted in the case (for more information on the Gibbard incident, see Leighton, 1977, and Lytwyn, 1990). According to oral tradition from Wikwemikong, Gibbard was murdered by a non-Aboriginal person after refusing to pay a gambling debt to another passenger (David T. McNab, personal communication, 1995).

Despite the spirit of paternalism offered by Whitcher and other government officials, the Wikwemikong, Saugeen and other Great Lakes First Nations preferred to control their own affairs. By 1863, however, the First Nations were in poor condition to assert jurisdiction over their aquatic territory. The government of Canada assumed jurisdictional control and, after Confederation in 1867, gave considerable powers to the province of Ontario. Comprehensive fisheries legislation introduced in 1857 appropriated most First Nations fishing grounds and leased them to non-aboriginal commercial fishermen. While purporting to be guided by principles of conservation and public safety, the fishery regulations enabled the government to give leases to fishermen who quickly over-harvested the resource. In 1876, Indian Agent William Plummer reported on the sad condition of the Saugeen Ojibway First Nation people who lived at Newash (Cape Croker). Plummer observed that "their fishing privileges are so curtailed as to be of little or no use to them. And I am afraid, in the approaching winter, that many of them, who cannot leave their homes and shift for a living elsewhere, will have to endure much hunger and privation" (Canada, SP, 1877, no. 11: 17).

In 1992, the Saugeen Ojibway First Nation (as represented by the Cape Croker Indian Band) engaged in a lengthy court battle with the Ontario government over fishing rights. In 1993, Judge David Fairgrieve ruled in favour of the Saugeen Ojibway fishermen who were on trial. He decided that the provincial fishing regulations were inconsistent with the existing aboriginal and treaty rights of the Saugeen Ojibway First Nation. However, Judge Fairgrieve did not succinctly address the issue of title to the fishing grounds or, more generally, to Lake Huron and Georgian Bay. He commented that, "In my view, it is again not a question of 'title' or 'ownership,' it is a question of the right to fish in those waters and to enjoy the benefit of the resource to be found there" (*R. v. Jones*, 1993: 477). Unfortunately, in declining to deal with the title issue, Judge Fairgrieve did not resolve the fundamental problem that has plagued the Saugeen Ojibway First Nation since 1836.

Conclusion:

Generations of government bureaucrats, lawyers, judges and scholars in Canada have assumed that lakes, rivers and aquatic resources belong to the Crown. That was also the prevailing view for many years regarding land and terrestrial resources until successful court challenges by First Nations demonstrated that aboriginal peoples held title to the soil. Two cases known as *R. v. Calder* in 1973, and *R. v. Guerin* in 1985, affirmed the existence of aboriginal title to land as being guaranteed by Canadian law. Thomas Isaac observed that:

Historically, Aboriginal peoples had their own forms of government, social organization, and economies. It is on this premise – that Aboriginal peoples have used and occupied these lands – that the doctrine of Aboriginal title, and subsequently Aboriginal rights, has developed. (Isaac, 1995: 1)

Court cases by First Nations challenging the title to aquatic territory have so far been unsuccessful. The landmark aboriginal fishing rights case in 1990 known as *R. v. Sparrow*, did not deal with the question of title to the water or the fishery resource. Although that case determined that there is an existing aboriginal right to harvest fish, it was the right to engage in the activity of fishing rather than the right to the fishery resource that was tried in court.

One has only to look at a map showing the locations of First Nations Reserves in the Great Lakes region to understand that water is essential to the livelihood and the identity of the people. The separation of land and water which is so common in the mindset of non-aboriginal Canadians, is not so discrete in the outlook of Great Lakes First Nations. Water and earth are perceived by aboriginal people as elements which combine to form part of the living world. It is evident from the historical records that First Nations who agreed to live on Reserves at the edges of the Great Lakes did not intend that they would be deprived of their livelihood and identity.

In the process of documenting aboriginal history relating to the "waterworld" of Great Lakes First Nations, it is evident that an artificial distinction has been drawn between the water and the land. Although well-suited to Euro-Canadian concepts of land ownership and riparian rights, this distinction does not fit well into aboriginal concepts about their territories. The Great Lakes continue to be an intimate part of the territory of the First Nations despite the delineation of boundaries and the enactment of laws and regulations imparting jurisdiction to other governments. It is incumbent on present and future scholars, lawyers and judges to appreciate that documents such as the *Magna Carta* are not the legal documents of the First Nations. We must strive to find the truth in documenting aboriginal history, and not perpetuate myths which have ill-served the aboriginal peoples of Canada.

References

Adney, Edwin Tappen, and Howard I. Chapelle
1964   *The Bark Canoes and Skin Boats of North America.*
        Washington, D.C.: Smithsonian Institution.

Anderson, Thomas G.
1847   "Evidence of Thomas G. Anderson given to a Special Committee to Investigate Indian Affairs, 1840," n.p., in: *Report on the Affairs of the Indians in Canada.* Ottawa.

AO, RG 1 Archives of Ontario, Crown Land Records, Toronto, Canada
1891   *Indian Treaties and Surrenders, Three Volumes.* Ottawa: Queen's Printer (reprinted in 1992 and 1993 by Fifth House Publishers, Saskatoon).

Canada, SP Printed Annual Sessional Papers of the Government of Canada, Ottawa.

Conway, Thor, and Julie Conway
1990   *Spirits on Stone: The Agawa Pictographs.* San Luis Obispo: Heritage Discoveries.

Eccles, W.J.
1984   "Sovereignty Association, 1580-1783," *Canadian Historical Review.* vol. 65: 475-510.

Fairgrieve, David (Judge)
1993   *R. v. Jones,* Written Decision of Judge David Fairgrieve, Ontario Provincial Division, 27 April, 1993.

Ferris, Neal
1989   "Continuity Within Change: Settlement-Subsistence Strategies and Artifact Patterns of the Southwestern Ontario Ojibwa, A.D. 1780-1861," unpublished M.A. Thesis, Toronto (North York): York University.

Havard, Gilles
1992   *La Grand Paix de Montréal de 1701: Les voies de la diplomatie franco-amérindienne.* Montréal: Recherches Amérindiennes au Québec.

Heidenreich, Conrad E., and J.V. Wright
1987   "Population and Subsistence," plate 18, in: Historical Atlas of Canada, Volume 1: From the Beginning to 1800. R. Cole Harris, ed., Toronto: University of Toronto Press.

Isaac, Thomas
1995   *Aboriginal Law: Cases, Materials and Commentary.* Saskatoon: Purich Publishing.

Lajeunesse, Ernest J.
1960   *The Windsor Border Region: Canada's Southernmost Frontier, A Collection of Documents.* The Champlain Society, Toronto: University of Toronto Press.

Leighton, Douglas
1977   "The Manitoulin Incident of 1863: An Indian-White Confrontation in the Province of Canada," *Ontario History.* vol. 69 (2): 113-124.

Lytwyn, Victor P.
1993   "The Usurpation of Aboriginal Fishing Rights: A Study of the Saugeen Nation's Fishing Islands Fishery in Lake Huron," pp. 81-103, in: *Co-Existence?: Studies in Ontario-First Nations Relations.* Bruce W. Hodgins, Shawn Heard and John S. Milloy, eds., Peterborough: Trent University.

Lytwyn, Victor P.
1990   "Ojibwa and Ottawa Fisheries around Manitoulin Island: Historical and Geographical Perspectives on Aboriginal and Treaty Fishing Rights," *Native Studies Review.* vol. 6 (1): 1-30.

NAC, RG 10
        National Archives of Canada, Department of Indian Affairs Records, Ottawa.

NAC, RG 68
        National Archives of Canada, Secretary of State Papers, Ottawa.

Nin.Da.Waab.Jig
1987   *Minishenhying Anishnabe-aki, Walpole Island: The Soul of Indian Territory.* Windsor: Commercial Associates/ Ross Roy Ltd.

Schmalz, Peter S.
1977   *The History of the Saugeen Indians.* Ontario Historical Society, Research Publication No. 5, Ottawa.

Trigger, Bruce G.

1985   *Natives and Newcomers: Canada's "Heroic Age" Reconsidered*. Montreal and Kingston: McGill-Queen's University Press.

Wallace, Anthony F.C.

1957   "Origins of Iroquois Neutrality: The Grand Settlement of 1701," *Pennsylvania History*. vol. 24 (1): 223-235.

Wright, Roland

1994   "The Public Right of Fishing, Government Fishing Policy, and Indian Fishing Rights in Upper Canada," *Ontario History*. vol. 86 (4): 337-362.

Oral Tradition on Trial

Paul Williams

British law used to love oral tradition. After all, it lies at the origin of ideas like "time immemorial" and is essential to understanding the system of common law. Gradually, though, as written statutes and written case law became the stock in trade of lawyers and judges, British oral tradition faded from favour.

If British oral tradition had faded, aboriginal oral tradition, in Canadian law, had been considered not worth the paper it was printed on. In the 1600s and 1700s British colonial and imperial officials conducted their business with Indian nations according to the laws and customs of those nations, and acknowledged the wisdom of those laws. By the 1820s that respect began to wane as the settler population increased and Indian nations became less valuable as military allies and less threatening as enemies.

Then, in 1982, the Ontario Court of Appeal decided the case of *The Queen v. Taylor and Williams,* also known as the "Bullfrogs Case." The court concluded that the oral tradition of an Indian nation was relevant in interpreting the treaties of that nation with the Crown. Though the judges did not say so, what they had done was create an exception to the "hearsay rule" – the rule that says that things one hears from someone else should not be accepted as evidence by a court.

In 1986, Judge Steele of the Ontario Supreme Court, in his decision in the *Bear Island Foundation* case (the case of the Teme-Augama Anishinabek), brought this new exception into sharper, narrower focus. He decided that Chief Gary Potts could not be a valid custodian of oral tradition because he did not speak fluent Ojibway and was not the son of any of the elders from whom he had learned the traditions.

Steele's decision, for aboriginal people, was the legal equivalent of getting hit by a truck and then having it back over you several times to make sure you were not moving. Higher courts overruled or retreated from many of its most damaging aspects. The matter of oral tradition did not come up in the appeals. No other Canadian court has considered the issue of oral tradition as valid evidence.

It had never occurred to me that oral tradition could be irrelevant. Unreliable, sometimes, it can be. Any person's evidence becomes unreliable over time and under the pressure of emotion, transmission, language shifts and distance. But judges are trained to sift the trustworthiness of witnesses. The reliability of oral tradition increases as the events are more recent, and with the particular skill and memory of its custodian. Some people are trained to remember. It is a skill that is less and less common in a society that has ever greater and faster access to stored information. Some people have learned to forget – a skill that has reached its apogee in modern federal and provincial bureaucracies.

To a person engaged in historical research, oral tradition is a vital resource. In almost every community I have worked in, the keepers of the oral tradition knew enough to guide me to the most important issues – my research was often a matter of finding and collating the papers that confirmed what these people already knew.

One of the real thrills of historical research is gathering the documents which, together, reaffirm the oral tradition. Some observers have called this a process of "validation" – which implies a presumption that without the paper the tradition might have been viewed as "invalid," or somehow second-class. That is wrong. The smile of an elder who sees his recollections confirmed is more than "I told you so." It contains the satisfaction of knowing that one's grandparents were right in what they said. It beams the equality of ways of remembering.

As a speaker for the Iroquois Confederacy explained to Crown representatives in 1736:

> We nevertheless have methods of transmitting from Father to Son, an account of all these things, whereby you will find the rememberance of them is faithfully preserved and our succeeding generations are made acquainted with what has passed that it may not be forgot as long as the earth remains.[1]

Two hundred years ago, there was a systematic way of ensuring that important things were remembered with precision:

> ...the treaties which they formerly made were oral & remembered by repeating them from father to son, but the memory is very much assisted by the wampum belts. When any foreign ambassador comes to them & makes any proposal they contrive to remember every word he says; different people are appointed to learn by heart a separate sentence & no more; so when they come to put it together they know every word of it.[2]

Even when aboriginal people learned to write, they still often chose to keep important transactions in their minds. There are important reasons for this; reasons which in this post-Gutenberg world we underestimate. The mind is still the most sophisticated recording and preserving device that humans have found. Its storage capabilities have not been fully tested. It is portable, does not need much temperature and humidity control, and is capable of complex storage, retrieval and correlation tasks. Knowledge stored in the mind can be transmitted or transferred to other minds, and that knowledge invests those other minds with abilities to use and understand the

---

1   Historical Society of Pennsylvania, Philadelphia, 1938.

2   New York State Library, Mss. #13350-51.

information. Most important, a matter that is kept in the mind is also kept *in mind*. Matters kept on paper are more easily stored and forgotten.

Rather than consider oral traditions in the abstract sense, I would prefer to give examples of my own experiences with them, as suggestions for things that legal and historical researchers sometimes overlook.

I remember Moses David in Akwesasne telling me: "The Ojibways, we Mohawks have a treaty with them. It says: 'we eat from the same dish.' It means the British has got to feed us both." Today, fifteen years later, I have a collection of documents from a dozen separate sources, each referring to a treaty between the aboriginal nations of North America that involves eating from the same dish or bowl. It owes its origin to a provision of the *Kaianerekowa* or Great Law of the Iroquois Confederacy, which says that the Chiefs will eat together from a single bowl of beaver tail stew. Its meaning is that the nations will share their hunting grounds; that hunting for food will always be permitted. There will be a single wooden spoon in the bowl – no knives or sharp edges are allowed, for this would lead to bloodshed.

The original wampum belt preserving this is now in the Royal Ontario Museum. I have seen documentary references to this "dish with one spoon" coming from as far south as the Creeks, as far north as the Crees, as far west as the Mississippi peoples. While I never did see any agreement that the British would feed both the Mohawks and the Ojibways, the Dish with One Spoon appears as a firm agreement between the Iroquois and the Ojibways during the eighteenth and nineteenth centuries.

Moses David also told me that the British had warehouses in Quebec City, full of presents and goods for the Indians – seven years' worth – and that all the Indians had to do was find the warehouses and ask for the presents, and they would be distributed. What I have found since is that an explicit treaty promise was made by the Imperial Superintendent General of Indian Affairs, Sir William Johnson, at the Treaty of Niagara in the summer of 1764. He promised that the King would always send presents to his Indian allies, "as long as the sun shone and the grass grew and the British worre red coats." The annual presents were delivered by the British Indian Department faithfully until the 1850s, and their gradual cutback and disappearance brought protests from many nations. There *were* warehouses for the presents at Quebec. Some goods were stocked up for seven years' worth of presents. Are the warehouses still there, waiting? I do not know – I have not been to Quebec to check.

Some years ago I met Dan Pine of the Ojibways of Garden River. Somehow our conversation turned to relations between nations, and he told me "there's people down south, we call them grandfathers. The place we came from, by the sea, they stayed there." Dan Pine said he had never met people of that nation. It took him some time to decide that these people were in fact the Delawares. It seemed strange to me that an old man in Sault Ste. Marie who had never met a Delaware would believe this. It was not until five years later, when I was reading a journal of Ojibway life in the late 1700s, that I found another clear statement that the Ojibways did indeed call the Delawares "grandfathers," and for precisely the reasons Dan had given. I had learned to be more careful, more respectful.

More recent events often carry with them more detailed recollections. If you speak with Ron Wakegijig of Wikwemikong about the 1862 "treaty" at Manitowaning, he can give you a precise account of what took place, in the words his grandparents taught him. If you read Wikwemikong's petitions and accounts of the transaction, all written in 1862 and 1863, the sequence of events is the same, and entire sentences of what people said are identical.

Nor should "oral tradition" be limited to people's recollections of stories and events. There is a song that is still sung at powwows on Manitoulin Island and the North Shore of Lake Huron which remembers that, of nearly three hundred Ojibway warriors who went to Niagara to fight for the British in the War of 1812, only six came back. Documents of the mid-to-late 1800s confirm this. Songs, too, form part of an enduring oral tradition.

Virtually every "land claim" or land rights issue that I know to have been accepted in Ontario has been the result of research that originated from what could be called "oral tradition." Vitually every researcher sets a list of priorities based on what the people have been told by their elders are their most important outstanding claims or issues. There is no magic to this: rather, it is exactly what one would expect in dealing with people whose cultures have not been based on the written word and whose grievances and rights have long gone unresolved.

There are some aspects of Ontario Indian oral tradition that remain unsolved mysteries. For example, everyone knows about the "Gunshot Treaty," and there are some documents purporting to explain that Lieutenant Governor Simcoe, in 1791, at Niagara or the Bay of Quinte, guaranteed that all Indians would always be able to hunt within the sound of a gunshot from any lake or river, and would be able to camp within sixty-six feet of their shores or banks. There is no written record of any such promise. There is a suggestion that land in the Bay of Quinte area was surrendered to within the sound of a gunshot from Lake Ontario, and there has been a practice of surveying a public allowance of sixty-six feet from the shores of lakes and rivers. The documents confirming the tradition of the "Gunshot Treaty," though, remain elusive. Maybe they do not exist – and maybe the Treaty was not as the tradition recalls.

To lawyers preparing aboriginal rights court cases at the end of the twentieth century, I suggest that basing a case on oral tradition alone is legal suicide, and ignoring oral tradition is also suicide. People's recollections of what has been passed down to them is a legitimate form of evidence that forms part of a balanced approach to presenting a case.

A well-balanced case today could begin with an elderly witness explaining what he has been told. In order to establish that this is indeed "oral tradition," the witness will explain whom he heard this from – often several different people in seveal places – and when. In some instances, it is very effective to have several witnesses, from several communities, each explain the same tradition. Certainly it is important to have more than one witness, and to have them explain that they have learned from several sources.

Then the oldest documentary evidence can be presented – and this should confirm, or at least be consistent with, the previous witnesses' statements. It is not uncommon for the original documents to agree with the oral tradition, but for there also to be some spillover, with each containing elements that the other does not. In the case of a treaty, the oral tradition might recall terms of the treaty that somehow did not make it into writing, or events at the treaty that were not seen by the Crown's representative.

Later documentary evidence follows. The courts have said that the conduct of the parties after a treaty is an indicator of their intentions at the time of the treaty. It is like ripples in the water – even if you no longer have the stone, the ripples often tell you that the stone has hit the water, and can often tell a trained observer much about the stone itself.

Finally, more modern historical analysis and commentary help fill in the gaps. Often a live historian or anthropologist can serve as an expert witness to explain aspects of what took place. Sometimes this is necessary to give the judges an understanding of the documents and words they have heard. In the "Bullfrogs" case, for example, the trial judge concluded that the Ojibways were impoverished because they said they could not speak as they should because their hands were empty. While they were probably indeed poor, what they meant was that they were not holding wampum. In the same case, when the Chiefs said that their wise old Chiefs were all dead now and they hoped the young men could do as well, the court concluded that they meant the important Chiefs had died in the War of 1812. Instead, someone who had read many treaty records would recognize the statement as a standard convention, used by speakers in treaties for at least two centuries. It is a statement of modesty and hope, and it could have been made at any treaty council. Of course, it is also possible that important Chiefs *had* died in the war, but the statement itself is not unique in Ojibway-British traditions.

In any historical research, but especially in seeking to record people's recollections, it helps to understand their language. Puzzling or problematic expressions in historic documents are often clarified in translation. For example, the difference between the French league and the British mile that lies at the heart of seveal claims around Lake Huron and Lake Superior is reflected in the fact that a single Ojibway word – meaning "a measure of distance" – can mean either a league or a mile. The unusual expression "Corachkoa our Great King" in the Nanfan Treaty of 1701 is resolved when one realizes that it is not the King's name but rather the Mohawk *Korahkowa*, meaning "the big Crown." And in the same treaty, "a place called

33

Quadoge," which has intrigued the mapmakers of the provincial government for some time, is probably not a problem any more once one translates "Quadoge" as "some place."

In the end, I believe that "oral tradition" is an inadequate word. In fact what we have been discussing is *knowledge*, and its distinguishing factors are two: first, that it was transmitted orally; second, that it was stored in people's minds. Both of these factors are different from knowledge transmitted in writing and stored in writing. Now that courts are beginning to accept other media – from computer disks to videotapes to hypnotic recollections to DNA analyses – as evidence, and are beginning to understand that each has its own strengths and weaknesses, it is easier for them to accept the first form of stored knowledge.

It is only a matter of time before the window created by "aboriginal oral tradition" will open wider in the courts, so that the knowledge of other peoples will also be seen as relevant and reliable evidence. And by then – if we are lucky – other peoples will realize, too, that keeping one's knowledge in one's mind is more than legitimate: it means keeping those facts and values *in mind*, so that one may remember and be guided by them.

Exploring Ojibwa History Through Documentary Sources: An Outline of the Life of Chief John Assance

Catherine A. Sims
Wilfrid Laurier University

When writing biographies of First Nations' leaders of the late seventeenth to the early nineteenth centuries, researchers are often confronted with difficulties stemming from the nature of their sources. The primary problem with documentary accounts is that government officials and missionaries generated most of these sources. Few First Nations' leaders living during this period recorded their thoughts in diaries, letters, or reports. In addition, the documentary record is often fragmentary and uneven. Yet opportunities for understanding the lives of First Nations' leaders exist by combining evidence in oral histories with that gleaned from documentary accounts. Documentary sources include the minutes of councils involving First Nations' leaders as well as other expressions of First Nations' perspectives. By examining the nature of key sources pertaining to one Ojibwa leader, Chief Assance, who spent most of his life in the vicinity of Lakes Simcoe and Huron, researchers can become familiar with the range of documents available for studying First Nations' leaders living in Upper Canada during the late eighteenth and early nineteenth centuries.

Knowledge of First Nations' languages provides fundamental insights into their culture and history. Assance's descendants, Merle Assance Beedie and Doris Assance Fisher, have indicated that the Ojibwa word "Assance" means "Little Clam." Assance was a member of the Otter Clan, a clan entrusted with knowledge of medicine.[1] The Ni-gig' or otter is significant to the Ojibwa Nation because the otter gave them "knowledge of the Four Sacred Directions" and "teachings about the Megis Shell," a crucial and initial part of the Ojibwa Midewiwin religion.[2] Throughout his life, Assance too was involved in teaching. Oral history indicates that he was a hereditary chief.[3] Many of his efforts were dedicated to instructing

---

1 Conversations with Merle Assance Beedie and Doris Assance Fisher, March 1989. I am grateful to Merle and Doris and to Elder Ernest L. Debassige for sharing their insights regarding Ojibwa history, culture, and language with me. I wish also to thank Merle Assance Beedie, William Assekinack, David McNab, and Dale Standen for their helpful comments regarding this paper and Donald Smith for sharing his research notes regarding Assance with me.

2 See Edward Benton-Banai, *The Mishomis Book: The Voice of the Ojibway* (St. Paul: Red School House, 1988), p. 66 and p. 71. Benton-Banai has also noted, "The otter is the one today who accompanies the newcomers into the Midewiwin Lodge. He accompanies them only through their First degree. Then they must part." (p. 65) See also Selwyn Dewdney, *The Sacred Scrolls of the Southern Ojibwa* (Toronto: University of Toronto Press, 1975), p. 26 and p. 46. I am grateful to William Assikinack for reminding me of the importance of the otter.

3 Conversations with Merle Assance Beedie and Doris Assance Fisher, March 1989.

Euro-Americans about the concerns, priorities, and needs of his people. Unfortunately, neither oral tradition nor documentary sources indicate when Assance was born.[4]

Government documents often provide essential insights into the involvement of First Nations' leaders with Euro-Americans. The Simcoe Papers, published by the Ontario Historical Society, are a valuable documentary source for exploring relations involving government officials and First Nations' leaders. Assance's early encounters with government officials stemmed from the government's desire to acquire Ojibwa lands. In the autumn of 1793, John Graves Simcoe, Lieutenant-Governor of Upper Canada between 1791 and 1799, explored the military potential of a harbour south of Matchedash Bay.[5] The Simcoe Papers reveal that the chief at Matchedash, whose name was not provided, gave Simcoe a present of twenty-four ducks.[6] Ojibwa oral tradition as well as documentary sources confirm that to the Ojibwa people, giving gifts was the most important means through which humans could communicate with the spirits and with each other. The present of ducks was more than a gesture of hospitality; for in Ojibwa culture, presents conferred responsibilities on the receiver.[7] Simcoe was impressed with the harbour at Penetanguishene. He believed that it could provide shelter if American armies occupied Detroit.[8] Government officials approached Ojibwa leaders living around Penetanguishene about ceding some of their lands in this strategically important part of Lake Huron.

The National Archives of Canada has microfilmed the originals of many treaties. A comparison of the originals of the treaties with the published versions

---

4   The Dictionary of Canadian Biography is an excellent beginning point for researchers investigating the lives of First Nations' leaders. Anthony Hall has indicated that Assance was born around 1790. This date, however, is not specified in documentary sources. See Anthony J. Hall, "John Aisance [sic] " in the Dictionary of Canadian Biography, Vol. VII, 1836-1850 (Toronto: University of Toronto Press, 1988), pp. 11-12.

5   J. G. Simcoe to Henry Dundas, 19 October 1793, in The Correspondence of Lieutenant Governor John Graves Simcoe with Allied Documents. Ed. E. A. Cruikshank. Vol. II. 1793-1794 (Toronto: Ontario Historical Society, 1924), pp. 90-91. Hereafter this work is cited as The Simcoe Papers. Simcoe was concerned with defending the colony against American attacks and interested in creating a naval station at Penetanguishene.

6   "Diary of Lieutenant Governor Simcoe's Journey from Humber Bay to Matchedash Bay in 1793 by Alexander Macdonell, Sheriff of the Homes District," in The Simcoe Papers, Vol. II, p. 74.

7   Conversation with Merle Assance Beedie, 18 April 1992. For a discussion of the significance of presents, see my "Algonkian-British Relations in the Upper Great Lakes Region: Gathering to Give and to Receive Presents, 1815-1843" (Ph.D. thesis, University of Western Ontario, 1992), pp. 1-22 and Charles E. Cleland, Rites of Conquest: The History and Culture of Michigan's Native Americans (Ann Arbor: University of Michigan Press, 1992), pp. 54-58.

8   John Graves Simcoe to Lord Dorchester, 14 March 1794 in The Simcoe Papers, Vol. II, p. 180.

of them reveals mistakes in the published renditions.[9] As well, the original versions of many treaties include the totems drawn by leaders; these totems can help researchers to trace the clans of First Nations' leaders. In May 1795, representatives of the Ojibwa Nation signed a provisional agreement. The description of the territory which the government wanted to acquire was vague, and the map accompanying the agreement illustrated the surveyor's unfamiliarity with the area (see Figure 1). Among those leaders listed on this agreement was "Keewaycamekeishcan" who used the otter totem as his mark (see Figure 2).[10] Doris Assance Fisher, an Ojibwa language teacher, has noted that " Keewaycamekeishcan" closely resembles "Keewaynakeishcan", meaning "He went in place of someone."[11] It is possible that someone represented Assance at the signing of this agreement.

The government took no immediate action to fulfill the terms of the provisional agreement. Simcoe left the colony in July 1796, and in his absence, Peter Russell became administrator of the Province. The Russell Papers, like the Simcoe Papers, provide worthwhile information about relations between government and First Nations and have been published by the Ontario Historical Society. The Russell Papers contain an account of a meeting at York in November 1796 involving two chiefs from Lake Simcoe and the Matchedash region. One of these chiefs was Assance. The chiefs reminded the commander at York of Simcoe's promises to provide them with assistance. Stressing that they had been neglected, one of these chiefs added, "Father I am sorry that we are thrown away. And that our Great Father Governor Simcoe should have a sweet mouth."[12] This message reminding officials of their promises and pointing out the discrepancies between the promises and actions of government leaders expressed themes which Assance emphasized throughout his life.

Government officials did not issue orders until October 1797 to send the goods for the Penetanguishene purchase to the Ojibwas of Matchedash and Lake Simcoe.[13] According to a treaty of May 1798, these Ojibwas ceded "a certain tract of

---

9   For a discussion of the problems associated with published versions of treaties, see Patricia Kennedy's "Treaty Texts: When Can We Trust the Written Word?" in *Social Sciences and Humanities Aboriginal Research Exchange/Échange sur la recherche Autochtone en sciences et humaines*, Vol. 3, No. 1, p. 1, 8, and pp. 20-25.

10 National Archives of Canada, Record Group 10, Vol. 1840, IT 019, Indian Affairs' Consecutive Number 5. Hereafter this collection of records will be referred to as NAC, RG 10.

11 Conversation with Doris Assance Fisher, April 1989.

12 "A Speech of Keubegon Onene and Escence to Major Smith, 25 November 1796," in *The Correspondence of the Honourable Peter Russell with Allied Documents Relative to His Administration of the Government of Upper Canada During the Official Term of Lieutenant-Governor J. G. Simcoe While on Leave of Absence*. Ed. E. A. Cruikshank and A. F. Hunter. Vol. 1. 1796-1797 (Toronto: Ontario Historical Society, 1924), p. 98.

land lying near the Lake Huron or butting and bounding thereon, called the Harbour of Penetanguishene." Assance drew the otter totem on this document (see Figure 3). The description in the treaty of the ceded territory was vague.[14]

Military records also provide information regarding the activities of First Nations' leaders. Assance fought against the Americans during the War of 1812. The Ojibwas from Lakes Huron and Simcoe participated at such locations as York where in April 1813, they helped to prevent American forces from capturing that fort.[15] Oral histories indicate that these Ojibwas also fought on the Niagara Frontier.[16] Records within E. A. Cruikshank's documentary collection of the War of 1812 specify that these and other Ojibwas from Lake Huron had encamped in July 1813 at the Cross Roads, three miles from Niagara. They engaged in skirmishes with the Americans who controlled Fort Niagara until 19 December 1813 when it was captured by the British and their allies.[17] In recognition of their service during the War of 1812, the chiefs of the Ojibwas from Matchedash and Lake Simcoe, including Assance, received medals from the British Crown.[18]

Government records regarding the Crown's acquisition of land from First Nations' groups also provide insights into the priorities of First Nations' leaders. After the War of 1812, the government's efforts to acquire more Ojibwa lands increased as the number of non-native settlers rose. In November 1815, Assance and two other Ojibwa chiefs drew their totems on a treaty ceding 250,000 acres stretching from Kempenfelt Bay on Lake Simcoe to Lake Huron. The treaty contained no reference to the blacksmith which these chiefs had requested at a council meeting with officials in June 1811. At this meeting, Assance had requested that his people

---

13 NAC, RG 10, Vol. 1, Indian Affairs, Upper Canada, Civil Control, 1796-1806, Robert Prescott to Mr. President Russell, 9 October 1797, p. 102.

14 NAC, RG 10, Vol. 1840, IT 017, Indian Affairs' Consecutive Number 5.

15 See Sir Roger Hale Sheaffe to Sir George Prevost, 5 May 1813 in *The Documentary History of the Campaign Upon the Niagara Frontier in the Year 1813.* Part I (1813) January to June 1813. Ed. E. Cruikshank (Welland: Tribune Office, 1902), pp. 187-188 and J. Mackay Hitsman, *The Incredible War of 1812: A Military History* (Toronto: University of Toronto Press, 1965), p. 124. See also Charles W. Humphries, "The Capture of York," in *The Defended Border: Upper Canada and the War of 1812*, ed. Morris Zaslow (Toronto: Macmillan, 1964), pp. 251-270. For maps and a chronology of the war, see *Atlas of Great Lakes History*, ed. Helen Hornbeck Tanner (Norman: University of Oklahoma Press, 1987), pp. 105-121.

16 Conversation with Merle Assance Beedie, March 1989.

17 See "Speech of Colonel Claus to the Indians," 12 July 1813 in *The Documentary History of the Campaign Upon the Niagara Frontier in the Year 1813*, Pt. II (1813) June to August 1813. Ed. E. A. Cruikshank (Welland: Tribune Office, n.d.), p. 260 and Thomas G. Ridout to Thomas Ridout, 20 June 1813 in *Ibid.*, p. 255.

18 Conversation with Merle Assance Beedie, March 1989.

be permittted to continue using their gardens at Penetanguishene.[19] But the treaty made no mention of the government's promise that the Ojibwas could continue to use their gardens at Penetanguishene until non-natives settled in the area.[20]

A rich documentary source of information for researchers studying First Nations' history is Record Group 10 of the National Archives of Canada. This group includes accounts of council meetings involving First Nations' leaders. One such meeting has not been discussed in the secondary literature. In July 1817, representatives of the reindeer, otter, catfish, and pike clans of the Ojibwa nation from Lakes Huron and Simcoe attended a council meeting at the garrison at York. James Givins, a superintendent of the Indian Department, explained that the King wanted more lands for European settlement. Assance's response to this request was significant because his speech raised themes which were important to this chief throughout his life. Assance began by explaining that the Ojibwas were united. He explained, "Father – Listen to what I am going to say [-] we are of one Nation." On behalf of his people, he requested a blacksmith and iron as well as fishing nets and hooks. He also urged the government to send a surgeon to attend the sick. Most significantly, he asserted that the Ojibwas would retain their hunting rights in the lands which they were expected to cede. Assance stated, "Father – We reserve to ourselves the right to beaver hunting and to hunting generally throughout the extent of Land which we relinquish to you. We request this because the Inhabitants are in the habit of destroying the Beaver when they happen to meet with their Huts." He concluded his remarks by declaring:

Father – Take courage. Do not allow us to be ill used by the people who are to be settled on the Lands which we sell you.

Father – I make known to you the manner in which those Persons who are on Lake Huron use us. When we go among them they take our Fish from us without paying us. [21]

---

19 NAC, RG 10, Vol. 1842, IT O62, "Proceedings of a Meeting with the Chippewa Indians of Matchedash and Lake Simcoe, 8 June 1811," p. 3.

20 NAC, RG 10, Vol. 1842, IT 047, Indian Affairs' Consecutive Number 16. See also Robert J. Surtees, "Indian Land Cessions in Ontario, 1763 -1862: The Evolution of a System" (Ph.D. thesis, Carleton University, 1983), pp. 176-177. For a further discussion of the background to and significance of this treaty, see Ian V. B. Johnson, "The Early Missisauga Treaty Process 1781-1819 in Historical Perspective" (Ph.D. thesis, University of Toronto, 1986), pp. 367-374. For a discussion of the processes involved in treaty-making with the Crown, see also David T. McNab, "Water is her Life Blood": The Waters of Bkejwanong and the Treaty-Making Process." Paper presented to the Laurier III Conference, 5 May 1994.

21 NAC, RG 10, Vol. 34, "Minutes of Council held at the Garrison of York on Saturday the 7th of June 1817, with the Rain [sic] Deer, Otter and Cat Fish and Pike Tries of the Chippewa Nation from the vicinity of Lake Huron," p. 19883.

39

This speech marked only the beginning of Assance's campaign to protect the natural resources of his people.[22]

Although government officials generated most of the correspondence regarding First Nations' communities, these letters often include the opinions of First Nations' leaders. For example, when Europeans wanted to cut hay in marshlands, Assance insisted that this part of his territory had not been ceded to the Crown. T. G. Anderson, a member of the Indian Department since 1815, reported that Assance had indicated that "when his ancestors sold the country they reserved the waters, Islands, and Game and that [as] the Hay was in marshy ground he claimed it as the produce of the water."[23] Assance believed that his people should be paid for any hay which outsiders cut from their lands. Throughout his life, Assance demanded that his people receive compensation when outsiders used their resources.

Missionary records are another valuable source for exploring the experiences of First Nations' leaders. Methodist missionaries worked among the Ojibwas living around Matchedash and Lake Simcoe (see map). Especially through the efforts of the Mississauga Methodist missionary Kahkewaquonaby, known also as Peter Jones, members of these groups became Methodists before 1830. Among his converts was Assance, the Matchedash chief whom Jones considered "a man of considerable thought and understanding."[24] The Ojibwa chief had converted to Methodism in 1827 and became known thereafter as John Assance.[25] Chief John Assance provided religious leadership for other resident Ojibwas. For example, when speaking of missionary activities among Ojibwas who lived just west of Penetanguishene, Jones remarked that several of these people had become Methodists "through the exhortations of Chief Asance [sic] and the class leaders."[26] Assance and other resident chiefs

---

22 Major James Givins, then a superintendent of Indian Affairs, promised to relay Assance's words to senior administrators. But the treaty of October 1818 did not mention hunting rights. Assance is not named in this treaty, and the otter totem does not appear on this document. See NAC, RG 10, Vol. 1842, IT 55, Indian Affairs' Consecutive Number 18, 17 October 1818. In earlier treaties, chiefs had requested fishing grounds to be reserved from the ceded territory. See, for example, NAC, RG 10, Vol. 1841, IT 038, Indian Affairs' Consecutive Number 13, 1 August 1805. I am grateful to David McNab for bringing this treaty to my attention.

23 NAC, RG 10, Vol. 46, T. G. Anderson to Col. J. Givins, 26 July 1830, p. 24178.

24 Peter Jones, *Life and Journals of Kah-Ke-Wa-Quo-Na-By: Rev. Peter Jones, Wesleyan Missionary* (Toronto: Anson Green, 1860), p. 73. Assance and Jones were related. See Donald B. Smith, *Sacred Feathers: The Reverend Peter Jones (Kahkewaquonaby) and the Mississauga Indians* (Toronto: University of Toronto Press, 1987), p. 108. Unlike many Ojibwa leaders, Peter Jones left a rich legacy including his autobiography, letters, and reports.

25 Victoria University, E. J. Pratt Library, The Peter Jones Collection, Box 1, File 1, p. 204. Unfortunately, Jones did not record Assance's age at conversion.

26 Jones, p. 232.

40

were not only influential in the conversion of their own people but also dedicated in their attempts to persuade visiting Ojibwas and Odawas to listen to the missionaries' messages.

Assance's loyalties to the Methodists were undermined, however, when he became convinced that the members of this denomination were linked to the radical reformer, William Lyon Mackenzie, and were, therefore, opposed to the Lieutenant-Governor.[27] In February 1832, he shared his fears with Bishop Alexander Macdonell regarding adversaries of Lieutenant- Governor Sir John Colborne:

> Father – As you are now going to York I wish to say a few words to you. I have heard, during the winter, many bad Birds – their voices are continually sounding in my ears. I now begin to understand them. I believe their object is to send away our Father at York. My heart is sore when I think of it. It is true I have not the knowledge of white people, but this I know if these bad birds should succeed what will become of us, the Indians? He has done us more good than any other father we have had at York. If my village was the only one concerned, (or even the Credit People) and all those below this, it might be of little consequence if we did suffer but, when I reflect on the great loss such a step would be to our Western brethren my heart becomes quite sore, and I wish you to tell my Father so [;] tell him also that I am now about rising up to prevent so far as I can so great an evil – tell him my voice shall soon be heard at a great distance.[28]

Assance decided to forbid a Methodist missionary from preaching to his people.[29] Throughout his life, Assance remained loyal to the British Crown, and his perceptions of the association between the Methodists and radical reformers contributed to his decision to abandon that denomination.[30] This speech also illustrates how Assance considered himself a spokesman for the Western Nations.

---

27 NAC, RG 10, Vol. 51, Indian Affairs, Chief Superintendent's Office, Upper Canada (Col. J. Givins) Correspondence, May - September 1832, James Currie to Reverend James Richardson, 16 April 1832, p. 56292.

28 NAC, RG 10, Vol. 50, "Substance of a Speech from the Chief John Aisence [sic] to His Lordship Bishop McDonald [sic] in Coldwater, 28 February 1832, pp. 55891-55892.

29 Ibid., p. 56291.

30 Other factors prompting Assance's decision to abandon Methodism included his association with such Roman Catholic leaders as Assekinack, Taibosegai, Taugaiwinene, and Ashagashe. See Sims, pp. 168-181. For a discussion of Methodist attitudes towards the rebellion, see Goldwin French, Parsons and Politics (Toronto: Ryerson Press, 1962), pp. 160-161.

Assance formally adopted Roman Catholicism in September 1832.[31] Frustrated in his efforts to prompt the government to address his people's grievances, Assance appealed to Roman Catholic church officials for assistance. The McDonell Papers at the Archives of the Roman Catholic Archdiocese of Toronto include transcripts of Assance's speeches. These and other papers within this archives contain references to many issues concerning First Nations. [32]

In 1830, the government began to create a model settlement at Coldwater and the Narrows. Officials attempted to entice Ojibwas living around Matchedash and Lake Simcoe to settle there and to become self-sufficient farmers and loyal supporters of the Church of England.[32] Because of the government's interest in this project, documentation regarding John Assance from 1830 to 1836 is richer than for other periods of his life.

Convinced that the Indian Department's scheme to create a model community had failed and aware that European settlers wanted additional agricultural land, Sir Francis Bond Head, Lieutenant-Governor of Upper Canada from January 1836 to March 1838, decided to terminate the experiment at Coldwater and the Narrows.[34] In 1836, he persuaded representatives of the Ojibwas of Lakes Huron and Simcoe to sign a proposal agreeing to cede lands "on the public high road leading from Coldwater to the Narrows of Lake Simcoe."[35] Assance and other Ojibwa leaders, however, later challenged the validity of this agreement. They appealed to Sir Charles Bagot, Governor General of British North America from 1841 to 1843, noting, "when Sir F. Bond Head insisted on our selling this Land and the bargain he had previously drawn out for us to sign, we were not made sensible of the full purport, so

---

31 Archives of the Roman Catholic Archdiocese of Toronto, Bishop Alexander McDonell Papers, AC 14.05, John Bell to Bishop McDonell, 2 October 1832, n.p. Hereafter this collection of documents will be cited as ARCAT, MP. I am grateful to Sister Frieda Watson, C.S.J. and to Marc Lerman of that institution for their assistance.

32 See, for example, ARCAT, MP, AC 07.06. "John Aisance, Speech to Bishop McDonald [sic]," 2 July 1833, n.p.

33 See Ian Johnson, "The Coldwater Experiment," Ontario Indian, Vol. 5, No.3 (March 1982), pp. 12-15, 22, 39, 56, and 58; Robert J. Surtees, "Indian Reserve Policy in Upper Canada" (M.A. thesis, Carleton University, 1966), pp. 97-132. For reproductions of contemporary sketches of the Coldwater settlement, Tony Hall, "The Politics of Indian Policy," Horizon Canada, Vol. 7 (Toronto: Centre for the Study of Teaching Canada Inc., 1987), p. 1988 and p. 1991.

34 For a discussion of Bond Head's views, see John Sheridan Milloy, "The Era of Civilization-British Policy for the Indians of Canada, 1830-1860" (Ph.D. thesis, University of Oxford, 1978), pp. 164-230.

35 NAC, RG 10, Vol. 1844, Indian Affairs' Consecutive Number 48, IT 126.

that we knew not the nature of the bargain."[36] Assance and the chiefs asserted that they had not received their annuity payments arising from the 1836 treaty.

Assance and other Ojibwas from Lakes Huron and Simcoe remained loyal to the Crown during the rebellions of 1837-8. Throughout December 1837, these Ojibwas were ready to march as soon as their services were required.[37] They responded to the call to arms from Sir George Arthur, Lieutenant-Governor of Upper Canada from March 1838 to February 1841, who wanted forces ready to defend the province against American border raids. Records of the British War Office, located in Manuscript Group 13 of the National Archives of Canada, include a paylist for those Ojibwas who remained on alert during November and December 1838 and January 1839. These eight chiefs and one hundred and forty warriors emphasized that they had delayed their trips to their hunting grounds because they were "always ready to serve their Great Mother when called upon."[38] After 1836, Chief John Assance led Ojibwas back to the Matchedash region, with most living on the nearby Beausoleil Island.[39] He died in July 1847.[40]

Throughout his life, Assance remained an articulate spokesman on behalf of his people, defending whenever necessary their interests and resources. Like the otter, he was dedicated to teaching. The clarity of his messages demonstrates that although problems arise from using documentary sources, these records, when combined with insights from oral history, can help researchers to learn about First Nations' leaders living in Upper Canada in the late eighteenth and early twentieth centuries.

---

36 Rama, Snake Island and Coldwater Indians to Sir Charles Bagot, 26 May 1842 in Florence B. Murray, ed. *Muskoka and Haliburton 1615-1875: A Collection of Documents.* (Toronto: Champlain Society, 1963), p. 115

37 NAC, RG 10, Vol. 124, T. G. Anderson to S. P. Jarvis, 7 January 1838, p. 69789 and Vol. 68, T. G. Anderson to S. P. Jarvis, 26 June 1838, p. 64592.

38 See NAC, Manuscript Group 13, War Office (London), Muster Books and Pay Lists. Militia and Volunteers, W.O. 13, Vol. 3693, "Paylist and Acquittance Roll of the Chippewas and Lakes Huron and Simcoe Assembled at Holland Landing for the Months of November and December 1838 and January 1839 – Under authority of His Excellency the Lieutenant Governor dated November 10, 1838", pp. 601-602. See also Andrew Borland to [Gerald] Alley, 20 January 1839 and Gerald Alley to S. P. Jarvis, 30 December 1830 in *Muskoka and Haliburton,* pp. 113-114.

39 Canada, Journals of the Legislative Assembly of the Province of Canada. From the 28th Day of November 1844 to the 29th Day of March 1845. "Bagot Commission Report," Appendix EEE, 1844-45, n.p.

40 NAC, RG 10, Vol. 408, Thomas Assance to T. G. Anderson, 12 July 1847, pp. 111-112.

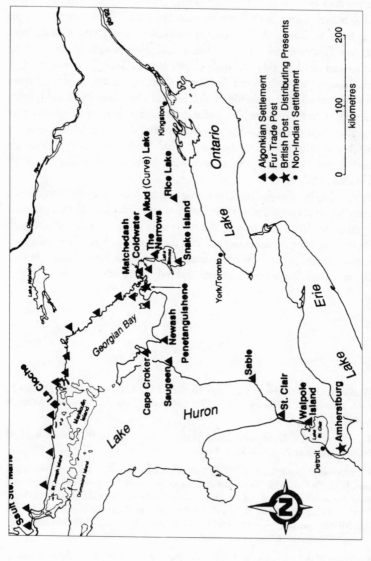

Selected Algonkian Settlements: Georgian Bay and Huron Regions, ca. 1835

Map by Gerry Box. Taken from Catherine A. Sims, "Algonkian-British Relations in the Upper Great Lakes Region: Gathering to Give and Receive Presents, 1815-1843," (Ph.D. Thesis, University of Western Ontario, 1992).

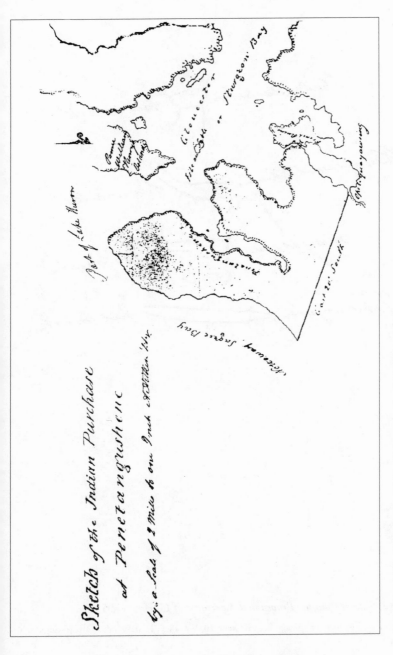

Figure 1: Map with the Provisional Agreement of 17 May, 1795

Source: National Archives of Canada, Record Group 10, Vol. 1840, IT 019, Indian Affairs' Consecutive Number 5

Figure 2: Totems from the Provisional Agreement of 17 May, 1795

Source: National Archives of Canada, Record Group 10, Vol. 1840, IT 019, Indian Affairs' Consecutive Number 5

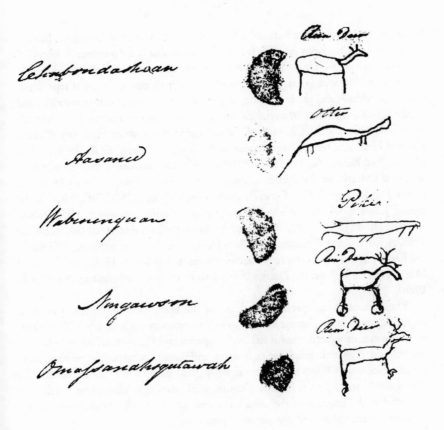

Figure 3: Totems from the Treaty of 22 May, 1798

Source: National Archives of Canada, Record Group 10, Vol. 1840, IT 017, Indian Affairs' Consecutive Number 5

History Without Writing:
Pictorial Narratives in Native North America

Joan M. Vastokas
Trent University

Visual representations have a crucial role to play in the writing of Aboriginal history, a role that so far has been insufficiently exploited. Available for purposes of historical reconstruction are the art works of both EuroCanadians and Aboriginal peoples.

Artists of European background provide us with an outsider's visual representation of individuals and group activities in portraits and scenes of community life, and of Aboriginal architecture, material culture, and natural environments. They have left us with representations of Aboriginal culture and events from an inevitably Western point of view. The best known records of this kind have been left by the Canadian painter, Paul Kane, who lived from 1810 to 1871 and travelled across Canada from southern Ontario to the British Columbia coast in the years 1846 to 1848 (see Figure 1 and Harper 1971). Others include John Webber (1752-1798), who accompanied James Cook on his Third Voyage to the Pacific (see Smith 1960:76-80); William Hind (1833-1888), who joined his brother's Labrador expedition as official artist in 1861; Peter Rindisbacher (1806-1834), who in his short career painted in the Red River colony in the early nineteenth century (Josephy 1970); and Edmund Morris (1871-1913) on the Prairies at the turn of the twentieth century (see McGill 1984).

The historian's interpretation and use of the watercolours, sketches, paintings, engravings, and, later, photographs, however, are not without a variety of difficulties. As in the case of written records left by Europeans and EuroAmericans in their various roles as explorers, missionaries, traders, militiamen, settlers, and tourists, these visual documents must also be used with great care as aids in the writing of Aboriginal history. This is because pictures, while aiming at descriptive "truth," are nevertheless the product of the artist's personal and culturally conditioned perceptions and interpretations of eye-witness experiences.

No matter how realistic in intention, all art works are "representations"; that is, they re-interpret what is seen, whether consciously or unconsciously. As a consequence, paintings, engravings, and even on-the-spot sketches of Aboriginal life have been shown to manifest whatever European attitudes prevailed at the time they were made. For example, in his pioneering monograph on the subject of cross-cultural representation, *European Vision in the South Pacific* (1960), the Australian art historian Bernard Smith shows how pictorial representations of Polynesian Islanders by European artists between 1768 and 1850 AD varied in both style and subject matter according to whether Europeans saw the Aboriginal islanders in a positive or a negative light and according to the European perceptions and aesthetic values of the time.

In the eighteenth century, for example, Polynesians were painted in the guise of classical Greek and Roman nobility, dressed not in their own native clothing, but in classical togas (see Smith 1970: Plate 52). By the nineteenth century, however, images of Pacific Islanders changed radically from "noble" persons to that of "ignoble" or even "wild savages" conducting practices of human sacrifice and massacre (Smith 1960: 243 and Plates 152-156). This turnabout in the representations, however, was not because of any change in the Polynesians themselves, but in the attitude of the European artists, which was to a large extent determined by the goals of evangelical missionary activity which sought to convert the indigenous peoples to Christianity. Depicting the Polynesians as savages served their propagandistic purposes. Such illustrations were widely reproduced in European missionary literature, which portrayed the life of Aboriginals in a negative light in order to justify their missionary activity and to make the case for the financial support necessary to continue their missions in the South Pacific.

A similar study by art historian Ellwood Parry on *The Image of the Indian and the Black Man in American Art, 1590 1900* was published in 1974. Visual representations by both painters and photographers were examined to demonstrate the fluctuating and often negative image of the Native American as well as the African American over some three hundred years of American history. At first, the Native American was depicted as a manifestation of the long-standing Western concept of the "Noble Savage." He was later represented as a savage murderer of innocent EuroAmerican women (Parry 1974: Figures 44-49).

At the same time, however, not all European artists painted such a negative, deliberately distorted picture of Aboriginal life and behaviour. Some, as in the case of John Webber, the artist who accompanied Captain Cook into the Pacific and to the West Coast of Canada in the late eighteenth century, aimed for a realistic "scientific" record of the Aboriginal communities he visited and left a body of valuable sketches, as did Paul Kane for the Canadian Prairies (Figure 2). Many of these artists' original drawings, more so than their finished paintings and engravings (Kidd 1950-1 and 1955), have proven useful in historical descriptions of Native village life at particular moments in time and in recording the appearance of important Chiefs and other Native leaders.

In using European art works as historical sources, however, one must become fully aware of specialized art historical knowledge as to both the techniques and ideology of visual representation. One must take into account the following deviations from "truthful" representation built into the very nature of artistic expression.

(1) Distortions in sketches made on the spot as a consequence of such factors as the artist's skill, style, perception, and culturally conditioned bias, as well as the aesthetic conventions in vogue at the time.

(2) Distortions in the art works as finished products, which result from the artists' catering to current artistic taste and fashion in order to sell his works in the market-

place (such as Neoclassicism, Romanticism, and Realism). The Romantics, for example, among whom we should count the finished paintings of Paul Kane, imposed dramatic light effects and exaggerated, often melodramatic, postures and gestures upon scenes of buffalo hunting and sometimes gave the faces of Chiefs and others the appearance of Greek and Roman sculpture. As well, portraits of Chiefs finished in Kane's studio on his return to Toronto sometimes included headdresses and costumes which did not belong to that particular individual, but which Kane may have seen and sketched on another individual in a different community or even Nation. The painting of an Ojibwa village at Sault Ste. Marie by Kane (Figure 1), for example, is based on a pencil sketch of the same subject, but with several human figures added (Figure 2).

(3) Distortions were also the result of European techniques of visual representation and reproduction. For example, an original pencil sketch or quick watercolour made on the spot by the artist, say John Webber, on his return to England would be handed over to an engraver for copying on to a plate for purposes of publication in multiple quantities for sale to the public or for reproduction as book illustrations. Not only would the final print or book illustration be reversed, but often the images were changed even further as a consequence of the engraver copying the original. Thus, the reader of the book or the scholar using these illustrations as historical "sources" would be viewing, at best, only a third-hand and much altered representation of Aboriginal life and culture.

Widely spread as such illustrations were among the European viewing and reading public from as early as the sixteenth century onwards, it is little wonder that the visual stereotyping and misrepresentation of Aboriginal peoples everywhere, their culture, their appearance, and their history took on such distorted proportions, culminating eventually in the historically questionable imagery of the Hollywood "Cowboy and Indian" movies of the twentieth century. The power of pictorial images as nonverbal systems of communication is overwhelming and of such a nature that art works can speak more loudly and more convincingly than the written word. Art works have a physical, sensate presence, giving an illusion of reality, such that the average person, untrained in the techniques of visual manipulation, may easily fall prey to the persuasive rhetoric of pictures.

Because the written word works its effect primarily upon the conscious mind, the reader of a text is mentally prepared to question whatever he or she is reading. In the case of pictorial images, however, communication is taking place at a deeper, unconscious level. Becoming aware consciously of the messages hidden in the work of visual art often requires considerable training to detect, the kind of training which schools and universities do not normally provide their students. The powerful effect of images as forms of nonverbal communication makes it necessary that scholars of

Aboriginal history investigate more deeply how visual images work upon the mind, the better to understand the role of pictorial images in history and their role in making history as well as their more commonly known function as depictions of historical events. Visual representations are useful documents only to the extent that the historian understands the sociocultural context of the artist and is familiar with the techniques and dynamics of artistic production.

But the problematics of using European pictorial images as sources for Aboriginal history are already well-known and there is an extensive body of literature on the subject dating from the mid-twentieth century onwards, when interest in Aboriginal history began to grow (for example, Hoffman 1960/61; Honour 1975; Hulton and Quinn 1964; Kidd 1950-51, 1955; McCracken 1959; Quimby 1954; Scherer 1975; Sturtevant 1980). In contrast, very little, if any, attention has been paid so far to the use of Aboriginal art works as a source for the writing of Aboriginal history from the insider's point of view.

There are a number of reasons why Aboriginal representations have been neglected in the context of an historical perspective (see Vastokas 1986/7 and 1992), but one stands out as the most relevant for discussion here. And that is the long standing perception by Euroamerican historians and art historians of Aboriginal peoples as societies without a history, let alone having any concern for the recording of their own history. It has been assumed that history is impossible without a system of writing, without the kind of alphabetical writing systems that record spoken language phonologically. Until very recently, European writers saw Aboriginal people in terms of an anonymous and static present. They perceived them as belonging to a state of nature more than to culture and as living in an eternal "cosmic" time rather than in a changeable historic time: decidedly not in a living stream of humanity unfolding towards an unknown and open-ended future. To all intents and purposes, it was common for many writers to consider that Aboriginal peoples had never even entered history and were merely relics of humanity's past.

As far as Aboriginal art works and Aboriginal history are concerned, what needs to be recognized first and foremost, is that Aboriginal art served not just one, two, or three, but very many different purposes in traditional culture and that new functions have been introduced since the arrival of Europeans to North America. It should be recognized at last that one of the most important functions of pictorial representation in traditional Native culture was the recording of history.

There are at least three, if not more, different ways in which Aboriginal artworks in North America may serve in the writing of Aboriginal history.

(1) Works of art as historical documents in themselves, that is, as physical objects with distinctive material and formal characteristics that exist in real space and real time and which are more or less datable and contribute, among other

things, to the development of historical chronologies (see Vastokas 1986-87:23-25);

(2) Works of art as cultural "expressions" (see Robb and Brown 1988), that is, visual embodiments of Aboriginal beliefs, values, and society. Using the skills of the "new," postmodernist art history, careful interpretation of the form, style, structure, materials, and subject matter of Aboriginal visual expressions provide skilful historians of art with knowledge and understanding of Aboriginal cultures both within particular historic periods and their changes over time; and

(3) Works of Aboriginal art as "representations" of events taking place in space and time, including such specifically historical events as migrations, tribal history, personal biography, and famous battles. Some comment is required here.

As indicated in an earlier paper (Vastokas 1984), Aboriginal art in North America may be divided into two fundamentally distinct functional categories, into "iconic" and "narrative" representations. In Western art historical usage, the term "icon" refers most specifically to sacred images which are revered in Christian and other religious spiritual practices. The term, "icon," however, may also be used to refer to depictions assuming the formal and functional character of icons, such as those of persons or entities of high status and power. Icons are generally static images, frontal, and symmetrical in composition. They rarely communicate any information whatsoever about a specific temporal moment or environmental location. Icons contain no landscape settings, no ground lines, and no attempt at perspective. Such iconic images dominate the iconography of North American Aboriginal art. They appear painted on West coast house fronts and Ojibwa and other Algonquian ritual drums (Figure 3) and constitute a majority of pictographs and petroglyphs throughout the continent. Iconic images consist of usually single images or symmetrical arrangements of three or more odd-numbered figures. The central figure in all cases is depicted in a frontal posture which signifies any or all of the qualities of authority, power and sanctity and by these means grips the viewer's attention in an almost hypnotic way.

But visual narratives are also a characteristic of many Aboriginal North American art forms. In contrast with iconic representations, narrative compositions are characterized by the co-occurrence of multiple motifs and elements which are disposed in a more perceptually scattered way than in icons. Such elements and motifs are so grouped as to suggest sequence and movement to the viewer's eye across the two-dimensional surface of their pictorial ground, whether that ground be a rock face, an animal hide, ivory, or a birch bark panel (Figure 4). Narrative structure and composition in Aboriginal North American art are most clearly exemplified in the birch bark scrolls of the Ojibwa peoples of the Great Lakes area. By means of sequential and directional elements, such as animal tracks; the depiction of environmental settings, as in ground lines, ground plans of lodges, the presence of trees, or by various lines suggesting movement left to right, upward, downward, or circular; both passage of time and movement across space are implied in the narrative structure of the pictorial bark scrolls. As in all visual narratives, profile animal and human images tend to suggest motion in one direction or the other, while frontal images imply momentary stops in action. In contrast to iconic images, visual narratives impose less of an hypnotic grip upon the beholder's attention, whose eyes participate more actively in the greater visual complexity of the narrative composition. This distinction between iconic and narrative representations has almost universal applicability in world art and, it is argued, is to be explained by the inherent nature of human response to visual imagery and to the psychology of art, rather than to the sphere of culture. As in the case of all visual narratives, the pictorial representations serve as mnemonic aids in the recitation of oral narratives. Because much Aboriginal oral tradition has been lost, it is only with the greatest of difficulty that these visual narratives may be employed in the writing of Aboriginal history. Nevertheless, they provide a challenge that is difficult for any art historian to resist. Given the cultural and spiritual importance of many such visual documents, however, progress in writing Aboriginal history may only occur by means of collaboration between elders who are the keepers of oral tradition and the scholarly techniques developed in the practice of art history, especially those methods employed in the study of ancient scrolls and illuminated manuscripts of Late Antique, Early Christian, and Mediaeval periods in the Old World (for example, see Weitzmann 1947).

An outline of research methods and resources available for establishing chronologies and for the interpretation of the function and meaning of art works in Aboriginal societies from prehistory to the present has already been presented elsewhere (Vastokas 1986-87). What requires further elaboration in the context of historical reconstruction, is the recognition that much of Aboriginal art was produced intentionally as "history" and of pictorial depiction as a Native American form of writing.

(4) Works of Aboriginal art as "Writing." Much could be said at this point about stimulating recent research into the origins of writing and of language and of the attention being paid to various forms of what is sometimes referred to as "pre-writing" and non-alphabetical writing systems. An important recent publication on literacy and writing in the Americas (Boone and Mignolo 1994:3) goes so far as to suggest that in Pre-Columbian America, art and writing are "largely the same thing," that we need to get away from the modernist Western conception of "art" as something to be appreciated strictly aesthetically and begin to address seriously the idea of visual representation as communication.

It is not for nothing that Native peoples have always and consistently referred to pictorial representations and to pictographs, in particular, as "writing." More and more, and especially since the successful translations of the Maya hieroglyphs over the past 20 years or so, scholars have renewed their interest in writing origins in general and in pictographic systems in particular, in both the Old and the New Worlds. In the case of Aboriginal North America, interest in the relationship between word and image implicates a tremendous variety of visual art works, including pictographs and petroglyphs painted and engraved on rocks and cliffs, to pictographs painted on Plains area buffalo hides, and depicted in such other media as Iroquoian Wampum belts. Perhaps most noteworthy in this respect are the pictorial birch bark manuscripts of the Ojibwa people of the Great Lakes region (Figures 4,5,6).

The Ojibwa birch bark records are associated primarily with the graded fraternity known as the Grand Medicine Society, or Midewiwin, devoted to both physical and spiritual healing and used in that context as well among the Menomini, Winnebago, and eastern Sioux. The records are required at every stage of the initiation to the society for both instructional purposes as well as ritual guidance and, in themselves, are considered to be sacred liturgical objects.

These bark records comprise an enormous array of pictorial representations which vary in form and imagery from depictive through symbolic, to entirely abstract in character. The pictorial representations are finely engraved with a bone stylus on the inner surface of the outer bark of the White Birch (Betula Papyrifera), which grows throughout most of Canada outside the Prairies and the treeless Arctic. Occasionally, the lines are filled with red pigment or, more rarely, blue, the two colours most frequently employed in Midewiwin symbology. The bark records measure from just centimetres to several metres in length, the longer specimens in the form of "scrolls" consisting of up to six separate sheets of bark stitched together with split spruce root or bast-cord made from the inner bark of basswood or cedar. For stability they are framed at two ends by wooden sticks about a centimetre or two in diameter. The bark panels inevitably curl into tightly wrapped scrolls, the form in which they are usually stored by their Ojibwa owners. The most important scrolls for historical as well as spiritual purposes are those which describe the origin, history, and rituals of the Ojibwa and of the Midewiwin society. These are the scrolls that are used by Mide members to record, narrate, and thus preserve their history and traditions. The bark records serve a vital role as visual narrative "texts," as pictorial mnemonic aids for the recitation of oral traditions. Individual scrolls may not be of very great age, but like the illustrated manuscripts of Early Christian and Mediaeval Europe, were faithfully reproduced when worn out or damaged or when additional copies were required by new initiates. As a consequence and in a certain sense, therefore, a particular scroll could be as "old" as several hundred years, as many Midewiwin leaders have claimed (see, for example, Dewdney 1975, Hoffman 1891, Landes 1968, Vastokas 1984, Vennum 1978, and Weitzmann 1947).

The pictorial bark manuscripts, it may be suggested here, serve as historical sources in all of four ways.

(1) As *documents in themselves*, that is, with their distinctive material, technical, formal, and stylistic characteristics as works of visual art produced at particular moments in time and space and exhibiting art historical relationships among themselves and with other pictorial traditions in Aboriginal North America. As such, the birch bark manuscripts belong to a much wider Aboriginal tradition of pictography on bark, wood, hide, and natural rock surfaces as practised especially among the Algonquian language speaking nations of North America whose territory extends from the eastern Atlantic seaboard throughout northeastern North America, the Great Lakes region, and the northern and northeastern Plains. Pictographs of a similar character are also known among their immediate neighbours, for example among the Iroquois, most notably in the form of Wampum "belts," and more distantly in evidence among the Thule period Inuit of Alaska and the Canadian arctic from about 1000 AD onwards, and extending into Siberia and Scandinavia, where similarly styled pictographs appear on the sacred drums of the Saami and in pictographs and petroglyphs on cliffs and boulders. Whether on bark, wood, bone, hide, or natural rock surfaces, the pictography in all of these regions exhibit differences but also similarities that suggest to the art historian a very widespread and ancient tradition of pictorial depiction that scholars have only barely begun to investigate with the seriousness and thoroughness the subject deserves.

Given their mnemonic function in the recitation of oral tradition within the context of the Midewiwin society, the Ojibwa bark scrolls have both a narrative and a liturgical function. They served, as well, both as permanent visual documents and as teaching aids for the education of newly initiated members of the society. As such, the scrolls vary in content and composition according to whether they illustrate traditions about the Creation of the world, the origin of the Midewiwin Society, about the Migration of the Ojibwa from the eastern seaboard to the headwaters of the Great Lakes, or about the structure and procedure of Midewiwin ritual in First, Second, Third or Fourth degree ceremonies. As well as these larger instructional and ritual scrolls, smaller oval-shaped song-scrolls served as mnemonic visual aids in the singing of Midewiwin songs.

Some writers have disputed the antiquity of the birch bark scrolls, suggesting that they, as well as the Midewiwin Society itself, are not Aboriginal in origin, but inspired by Christian ritual and symbolism (for example, Hickerson 1962, 1970). This suggestion, however, cannot be taken seriously by the art historian owing, firstly, to the weakness of their argument (which sees a resemblance of the fourth degree four-quarter's symbol to the Christian cross and to the complexity of the society itself as incompatible with a hunting-gathering way of life), and secondly, to the abundant evidence available on the antiquity and wide dissemination of pictorial narratives among Pre-Columbian peoples in general, including of course, those of the Maya, Aztec, and Mixtec peoples of Mesoamerica. The lack of recognition and acceptance by scholars of the Ojibwa sacred scrolls as indigenous in origin has so far inhibited their investigation in art historical depth. With a few exceptions, almost all of this research lies still in the future.

(2) This is also true of Ojibwa narrative scrolls as *cultural expressions*. What is still lacking is an overall investigation of the pictorial conventions employed in the scrolls in relation to Ojibwa culture and world view. I am referring in particular to the more ephemeral and latent aspects of culture – such as concepts of space and time, being and becoming, transformation between the seen and the unseen and interface between the spiritual and natural realms – as revealed in the composition of specific elements within the pictorial narratives and the various devices employed in them for the depiction of space, time and movement. In an earlier paper (Vastokas 1988), the underlying compositions of these remarkable documents of liturgical art were explored as expressions of Ojibwa concepts of space and time and as visual narratives grounded in Ojibwa oral tradition, thought, and everyday experience. For example, formal analysis revealed a basic ordering principle in all of the pictorial scrolls, despite their great variety. This was found to be either an explicit or implicit line or "path" that makes its way across the surface of the bark, a line that most often moves from right to left, that is, from East to West. The line may be straight or curved, go round in a spiral or circle, in which latter case the directional movement is clock-wise or, more fundamentally, sun-wise. The line may be interrupted and it may take detours. The biographical and tribal histories painted on Plains area buffalo robes, for example, in which pictorial elements are arranged spirally from inside outward, visualize a similarly fundamental linear progression in time and space.

This visually depicted or merely implied line, of course, is symbolic of the "Path of Life" and of the moral code of the Ojibwa people as described by medicine-man James Red Sky (1972:90):

When God created the world, in the beginning He set aside a path of life. Human beings could choose to follow this path in order to gain everlasting life. If this path had not been set aside, His people would have been disorganized and this would have resulted in the destruction of mankind. Everything would have been wiped from the face of the Earth.

In Ojibwa world view, it is this line that holds everything live in the world together.

(3) As *representations* of events taking place over time and in space, the birch bark scrolls also function as records of Aboriginal history. This is most evident in the so-called "Migration Scrolls" (Figure 6), which illustrate the route of Ojibwa migration from the Atlantic seaboard, up the Saint Lawrence River, and through the various

Great Lakes, to northwestern Ontario, Minnesota, Wisconsin, and eastern Manitoba. Symbolic elements, such as a set of wavy lines within a rectangle in some examples, signify such specific locations as the rapids at Sault Ste. Marie. Migration scrolls do not aim, like modern maps, for optical and mathematically measurable accuracy, but are intended to serve as visual cues for the oral narration of an historical event. In this way, the spoken word and the visual image function together in the larger context of narrative performance during instruction or during ceremonials.

(4) And finally, we must begin to re-examine Ojibwa bark scrolls as a form of *"writing without words."* As argued recently by Elizabeth Boone and Walter Mignolo (1994), the terms "art" and "writing" are very problematic for Aboriginal America. Unlike Western and other alphabetical writing systems, the goal in the Americas was not "visible speech." For Pre-Columbian Americans, "art and writing ... are largely the same thing." Alphabetical writing, they point out, is not the only form of writing known to the world. They distinguish clearly between "glottographic" (or phonetic) writing systems which do aim at representing speech, and "semasiographic" writing systems which communicate ideas independently of language. Ojibwa bark scrolls, it may be suggested, belong to the latter. Among these semasiographic writing systems a subset of "iconic" writing systems is recognized, which consists largely of representational pictographic elements which "convey meaning without a detour through speech." Aztec and Mixtec writing, they argue (p. 18), constitute such iconic semasiographic writing systems wherein "meaning is carried by pictorial and conventionalized images, by their relative placement, and by the contexts in which they participate." Such systems "are intelligible to those who share a general cultural base even though they might speak different languages." In these kinds of systems, write Boone and Mignolo, "the pictures are the texts. There is no distinction between word and image." Their conclusion as to the Aztec and Mixtec writing systems, one could easily argue, is equally applicable to the pictorial narratives of the Ojibwa:

> One thing shared by all these indigenous New World systems is that they give accountability. Because they are permanent, or relatively so, they functioned for their societies to DOCUMENT and to ESTABLISH IDEAS. As RECORDS, they are memory that can be inspected by others ... all were accepted as valid documents (Boone and Mignolo 1994: 22)

The Ojibwa birch bark scrolls are among a variety of visual narratives offering both Aboriginal and EuroCanadian historians an insider's perspective on Native American history. Interpreting these Aboriginal documents, however, is no less problematic to the historian than the visual records left by the European outsiders. They merely present a different set of historical challenges, the most obvious of which being the absence of absolute dating. Research is also needed into the oral traditions accompanying these visual records and into the ritual and sociocultural contexts in which they were employed. Very few elders remain who are still fully in touch with these traditions. Much has been lost, but also much remains. The challenge for both Native and non-Native historians of Aboriginal history is great but promises great rewards if they pursue their task cooperatively with diligence, openness, new skills, and inter-disciplinarity from both inside and outside the Native perspective.

References

Boone, Elizabeth Hill and Walter D. Mignolo (eds)
1994   *Writing Without Words: Alternative Literacies in Mesoamerica and the Andes.* Durham and London: Duke University Press.

Dewdney, Selwyn
1975   *The Sacred Scrolls of the Southern Ojibwa.* Toronto: University of Toronto Press.

Harper, J. Russell
1971   *Paul Kane's Frontier.* Austin and London: University of Texas Press.

Hickerson, H.
1962   Notes on the Post-Contact Origin of the Midewiwin. *Ethnohistory* 9: 404-423.
1970   *The Chippewa and Their Neighbors: A Study in Ethnohistory.* New York: Holt, Rinehart and Winston.

Hoffman, B.G.
1960/1   The Codex Canadiensis: An Important Document for Great Lakes Ethnography. *Ethnohistory* 7-8: 382-400.

Hoffman, W.J.
1891   The Midewiwin or 'Grand Medicine Society' of the Ojibwa. *Seventh Annual Report of the Bureau of American Ethnology for the Years 1885-1886.* Washington, D.C.

Honour, Hugh
1975   *The New Golden Land: European Images of America from the Discoveries to the Present Time.* New York: Pantheon Books.

Hulton, Paul and David Beers Quinn
1964   *The American Drawings of John White, 1577-1590.* Two Volumes. London: The Trustees of the British Museum.

Josephy, Alvin M.
1970   *The Artist Was a Young Man: The Life Story of Peter Rindisbacher.* Fort Worth: Amon Carter Museum of Western Art.

Kidd, Kenneth E.
1950-51   Paul Kane - A Sheaf of Sketches. *Canadian Art* 8: 166-167.
1955   Paul Kane, Painter of Indians. *Royal Ontario Museum of Archaeology, Bulletin 23* (Toronto), pp. 9-13.

Landes, Ruth
1968   *Ojibwa Religion and the Midewiwin.* Madison: University of Wisconsin Press.

MacLeod, Margaret A.
1945   Peter Rindisbacher: Red River Artist. *Beaver*, Outfit 276, pp. 3036.

McCracken, Harold
1959   *George Catlin and the Old Frontier*. New York: Bonanza Books.

McGill, Jean S.
1984   *Edmund Morris: Frontier Artist*. Toronto and Charlottetown: Dundurn Press.

Parry, Ellwood
1974   *The Image of the Indian and the Black Man in American Art, 1590-1900*. New York: George
            Braziller.

Quimby, George I.
1954   *Indians of the Western Frontier: Paintings of George Catlin*. Chicago: Chicago Natural
            History Museum.

Rabb, Theodore K. and Jonathan Brown (eds)
1988   The Evidence of Art: Images and Meaning in History. In: *Art and History: Images and Their
            Meaning*, pp. 1-6. Edited by Robert I. Rotberg and Theodore K. Raab. Cambridge:
            Cambridge University Press.

Red Sky, James
1972   *Great Leader of the Ojibway: Mis-quona-queb*. Edited by James R. Stevens. Toronto:
            McClelland and Stewart.

Scherer, Joanna C.
1975   Pictures as Documents: Resources for the Study of North American Ethnohistory. *Studies in
            the Anthropology of Visual Communication* 2 (2): 65-79.

Smith, Bernard
1960   *European Vision in the South Pacific, 1768-1850: A Study in the History of Art and Ideas*.
            Oxford: Clarendon Press.

Sturtevant, William C.
1980   Patagonian Giants and Baroness Hyde de Neuville's Iroquois Drawings. *Ethnohistory* 27(4):
            '331-348.

Vastokas, Joan M.
1984   Interpreting Birch Bark Scrolls. *Papers of the Fifteenth Algonquian Conference*. Edited by
            William Cowan. Ottawa: Carleton University. pp. 425-444.

1986/7   Native Art as Art History: Meaning and Time from Unwritten Sources. *The Journal of
            Canadian Studies* 21 (4): 7-36.

1988   Space and Time in Algonkian Birch Bark Records: The Case for Narrative Art in Native
            North America. Paper read at the March 1st meeting of the Native Art Study Group of
            Ottawa, Ottawa, Ontario.

Vennum, T.
1978   Ojibwa Origin-Migration Songs of the Midewiwin. *Journal of American Folklore* 91:
            753-793.

Weitzmann, K.
1947   *Illustrations in Roll and Codex: A Study of the Origin and Method of Text Illustration*.
            Princeton: Princeton University Press.

Figure 1: Ojibwa Village, Sault Ste. Marie.

Painting by Paul Kane, 1845. Oil on canvas, 48 cm x 76 cm.

Royal Ontario Museum, Cat. No. 912.1.9 Photograph Courtesy of the Royal Ontario Museum, Toronto.

This finished work by Kane is based upon the original pencil sketch shown in Figure 2, but with human figures added.

Figure 2: Ojibwa Village, Sault Ste. Marie.

Drawing by Paul Kane, 1845. Pencil on paper, 14.6 cm x 22.2 cm.
Royal Ontario Museum, Cat. No. 946.15.21. Photograph Courtesy of the Royal Ontario Museum, Toronto.

61

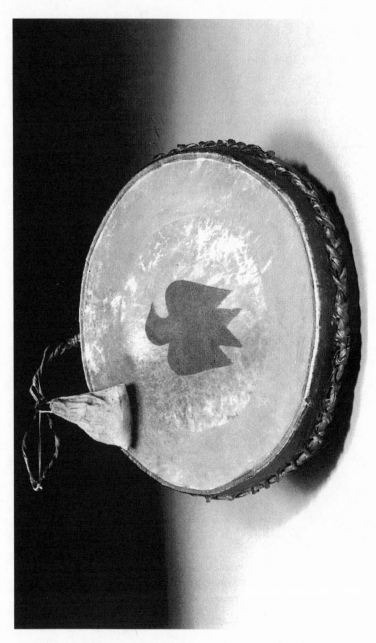

Figure 3: Shaman's Drum.

Ojibwa, late 19th century, Rawhide, wood, paint, 5.3 x 32.2 cm.
Canadian Museum of Civilization, Ottawa, Cat. No. III-G-898.
Example of an "iconic" representation, characterized by symmetry, frontality, and compositional simplicity.

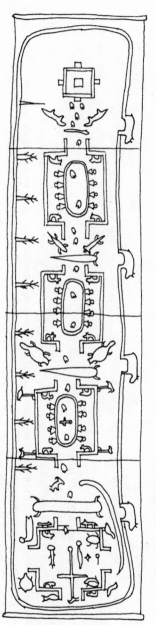

Figure 4: Ritual Scroll.

Ojibwa, date unknown. Birch bark, 1.8 m L. Tracing after Dewdney 1975: Figure 73, page 92.

Example of a "narrative" representation, characterized by compositional complexity, multiplicity, and directional arrangement of visual elements, used to accompany oral narrative outlining correct ceremonial procedure to initiates.

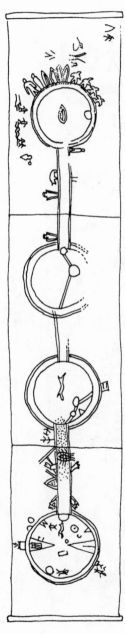

Figure 5: Creation Scroll.

James Red Sky Senior, Ojibwa, Shoal Lake, Ontario; date unknown. Birch bark, 1.4 m L. Glenbow Museum, Calgary, Cat. No. AP 500b. Tracing after Dewdney 1975: Figure 36, page 49.

Another visual narrative describing the Ojibwa story of Creation as recorded and taught by the late James Red Sky Senior, Midewiwin Master.

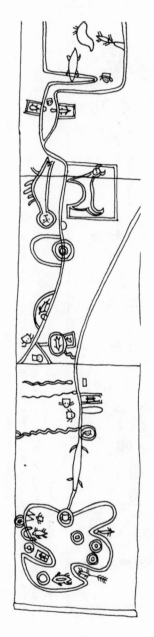

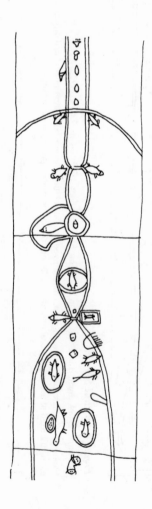

Figure 6: Migration Scroll (detail).

James Red Sky Senior, Ojibwa, Shoal Lake, Ontario; date unknown.
Birch bark, 2.6 m L. Glenbow Museum, Calgary, Cat. No. AP 500c. Tracing after Dewdney 1975: Figure 47, pages 62-63.

This visual narrative records and describes the Ojibwa legend of migration from the place of origin in the East, up the St. Lawrence River and lower Great Lakes to the headwaters of Lake Superior. Scrolls are normally read from right to left (east to west).

Appendix

Documenting Aboriginal History in Ontario

A Symposium sponsored by the Champlain Society
with the assistance of the Ministry of Culture, Tourism
and Recreation of the Government of Ontario*

hosted by Nin.Da.Waab.Jig
Walpole Island First Nation Heritage Centre

September 23, 1994

Morning Session

8:30 am   Registration

9:00 am   Welcome and Introduction
          Joseph Gilbert, Chief, Walpole Island First Nation
          Professor Gerald Killan, King's College, London, Ontario,
             President of the Champlain Society

Oral Tradition and Aboriginal History

Chair: Professor Bryan Loucks,
          Walpole Island First Nation and Trent University

Participants:
          Bernita Brigham, Walpole Island First Nation,
             Yes is Better than No.
          Dean Jacobs, Executive Director, Nin.da.waab.jig, Walpole Island
             First Nation, *"We have but our hearts and the traditions of our
             old men": Understanding the Traditions and History of
             Bkejwanong.*
          Victor Lytwyn, Ph.D., Historical and Geographical Consulting
             Services, *Waterworld: The Aquatic Territory of the Great Lakes
             First Nations.*

---

* Currently the Ministry of Citizenship, Culture and Recreation.

Afternoon Session

1:30 - 3:30 pm

The Diversity of Aboriginal History

Chair: Professor Sylvia Van Kirk, University of Toronto

Participants:

Joan Vastokas, Trent University, *History Without Writing: Pictorial Narratives in Native North America.*

Catherine A. Sims, Wilfrid Laurier University, *Exploring Ojibwa History Through Documentary Sources: An Outline of the Life of Chief John Assance.*

Neal Ferris, Ontario Ministry of Culture, Tourism and Recreation, *Archaeology as Documentation of Aboriginal History in Ontario.*

4:00-6:00 pm Boat tour of Bkejwanong, Walpole Island

Evening Session

7:00 pm   Dinner, Walpole Island Cultural Community Centre

Guest Speakers:

William Tooshkenig, Association of Iroquois and Allied Indians, *Introduction.*

Keynote Address

William Assikinack, University of Regina,
The Need to Interpret/Validate Oral Aboriginal His/Her Story.